DADDY DAYS!

Daddy Days!

A Recipe for a Life of Adventure and Better Relationships with Your Children, Family, and Friends!

By John Turner with Jay Bouchard

Peter E. Randall Publisher
Portsmouth, New Hampshire
2025

ISBN: 9781942155959
Library of Congress Control No. 2025913678

Published by
Peter E. Randall Publisher
5 Greenleaf Woods Drive, #102
Portsmouth, New Hampshire 03801
www.perpublisher.com

Book Design: Tim Holtz

Printed in the United States of America

Contents

PART 3
DOING HARD THINGS

PART 4
MARRIAGE

PART 5
EVOLUTION

Introduction by Jay Bouchard

Around every bend in the trail, I expected to see a sign indicating we'd reached our campsite, or that we were getting close, or that, at the very least, we were hiking in the right direction toward a destination that did, in fact, exist. But as the path meandered endlessly uphill, each step carried with it a modicum of disbelief. Surely, we should have arrived already.

The sun was setting. Maybe it already had. It's sometimes hard to know in the woods of northern New Hampshire where maple and pine canopy offers only fleeting views overhead. When you're below tree line in a boreal forest, especially on a cloudy day, the sun's exact whereabouts do not matter much—that is, until the sun disappears altogether. We were approaching that hour, hiking in the near darkness that awakens mosquitoes and makes weary travelers wonder why in God's good name they're still plodding along.

In this instance, I knew why. It was 2010 and I was walking in the footsteps of John Turner.

I'd known John for much of my childhood. My brother and I attended the same Catholic grade school as his children, the now-closed Villa Augustina. We had lived in the same town, Goffstown, the kind of place where most people know most people. And while I didn't know John intimately, I knew his reputation as a man of incessant adventure—always moving, always hiking, always skiing. His energy was frenetic, a secondhand observation I'd gleaned from my brother, who had joined John's family on adventures to the coast of Maine, up Tuckerman Ravine on Mount Washington, and on a biking tour along the Hudson in New York City.

My earliest memory of John came, quite literally, in passing. One year, he was running the Goffstown Gallop, a 5.2-mile course that wends around town, carrying runners up and down hills before depositing them in a parking lot near my childhood home. My dad brought me to a spot near the finish line as runners, most of whom looked beaten, shuffled past. And then came John running by us, sporting an inexplicably wide smile. My dad remarked that only John Turner could look so happy doing something so grueling. Back on that trail in northern New Hampshire, as my spirit faded with the daylight, I remembered the wide smile on John's face and I realized, even in this moment, he was having the time of his life.

We were somewhere east of the town of Jefferson below Mount Cabot. Earlier in the day we'd climbed Mount Waumbek with a plan to traverse from one summit to the next and make camp. Each mountain was on the New Hampshire Four-thousand Footer list, encompassing forty-eight peaks in the state with summits higher than four thousand feet. At age seventeen, I'd been crossing peaks off that list over the course of several years, as had John and his oldest daughter, Maria, which is why our families planned this trip together. But when we got to the summit of Waumbek, we found an impassable traverse. Downed trees and a lack of maintenance meant we would have to turn back, descend to our cars, and drive to a different trailhead to begin our next ascent.

By the time we hiked down, shuffled vehicles, and started the climb toward our eventual camp, dusk was nearly upon us. If it was up to me, we would have car camped and set off for the summit of Cabot the next morning. But this was a John Turner expedition, and as I would learn, his enthusiasm is exceeded only by his determination to share an adventure with his kids. There would be no half measures.

Our crew numbered ten, ranging in age and experience, including my brother and my dad, John's three kids, and a few Turner cousins. John's youngest daughter, Cecilia, who at the time was only nine, wailed as the miles accumulated beneath our boots. If there was a silver lining, it was that her protests scared off any black bear or moose that might have given us trouble. While John lingered to nurture her, he made sure the entire group kept moving.

After a few miles, the campsite finally appeared next to a small pond, into which John and his kids instinctively plunged. When he emerged from the water dripping, he was wearing a wide smile—one I recognized, and one that assured me no matter how hard the day had been, it was worth it for him—because of the quality time spent with children and loved ones.

Front row (l to r) Maria, Carlos, Cecilia, and co-author Jay Bouchard. Back row (l to r) Jay's dad Gary Bouchard, John Turner, Derek Russell, Phil Bouchard, and Alysia Delgado-Sorce.

In the years to follow, John and I ran into each other only sparingly around town and at holiday parties, owing mostly to my leaving New Hampshire for college in Montana. Though I always figured I'd return, a career in the magazine industry brought me to Chicago, Santa Fe, and eventually Denver, where I still live. Then, in the fall of 2024, about a month before my wife and I welcomed our first child into the world, John got back in touch. He was writing a book about fatherhood, he told me. Much of it was already written and he was looking for an editor, maybe even a co-author, someone who could help shape his voice, structure themes, and bring to life a concept in his family known as "Daddy Days."

As we discussed the project, we realized how much we share in our adult lives. We are both skiers, sailors, and general-interest outdoorsmen who practice the same faith and believe in the same promise of strong relationships. When John learned I was soon to become a father myself, he found the news downright providential. He had been spending months reflecting on his journey as a parent; mine was about to begin. He'd seen it all; I'd seen nothing yet.

When I read the earliest draft of this book, it occurred to me John was attempting to thread a needle between memoir and parenting advice, a guidebook of sorts framed by the countless "Daddy Days" he shared first with his father and later with his own children. He stressed to me early on he was not trying to write a memoir, that he was no greybeard reflecting on a life well lived. Nonetheless, the advice he wanted to impart was inextricably tied to the arc of his life and the many stories shaped by his unyielding zeal for the next family adventure.

Over six months, we wrestled with this tension, forming chapters in such a way that readers would understand what makes John Turner tick. And, more importantly, how he and his wife, Renée, raised a family that stayed in constant motion, and how the lessons of countless "Daddy Days" will help fathers everywhere forge deeper bonds with their kids. John, an engineer by trade, emphasized constantly his goal was to give dads a blueprint to build something permanent. Though I may not have realized it initially, he was giving me early access to that blueprint, too.

There were moments in the creation of this book when John and I were transported back to the trail below Mount Cabot. Though we were moving with purpose, we feared at times our destination might not appear around the next bend, nor the one after that. As our deadline with the publisher neared, we knew the sun was setting and that only with a hurried pace might we make it. But, as I've come to learn, this is a natural state of being for John Turner, a zone where he comes alive and pushes those beside him to the finish line. Sure enough, following his lead, we made it before the dark descended. The campsite appeared. The pond beckoned. This time, we'd both jump in.

Preface by John Turner

The alarm clock breaks my sleep at 4 A.M. on April 25, 2009. Less than an hour later, we are in the middle of the New Hampshire woods. Sunrise will not be until almost 6 A.M. It's dark, chilly, and silent as we sit on the forest floor waiting to hear a turkey gobble. My ten-year-old son, Carlos, is near me, shotgun at the ready. Our friend and hunting coach, Dwayne, occasionally scrapes a yelp—mimicking a hen's voice to let the gobbler know she's ready to mate.

We wait. The air is still. The eastern sky reddens as the sun approaches the horizon, and for the first time since we crouched in these woods, the birds forget our presence and start to chirp. Bluejays, chickadees, sparrows, and robins sing. Though I've never been a hunter, I begin to understand the appeal as the forest comes alive. Dwayne scrapes out another yelp, and just as he predicted, we hear our first gobble. My heart pounds with joy and anticipation—and with excitement for my son. We'd been talking about this moment for months. We attended hunter safety classes together. We purchased the gear. And now the climax approaches.

Soon, the turkeys jump out of the tall pine trees, beating their wings as they fall to the ground. Thump. Thump. Thump. We hear as the birds hit the soft forest floor. Carlos is resolute, handling all of this like a man. He is completely focused on what is happening around us. He is following Dwayne's instructions perfectly as he remains silent and stationary but attentive and observant. I just sit there, praising God for letting us experience this together.

Another yelp call by Dwayne and, sure enough, the gobbler is intrigued. I don't see him, but I can hear the careful footsteps as he is drawn toward us. We wait. Carlos is the hunter of the day. It is his responsibility to decide if and when he has a clean shot. A good hunter is respectful of nature. A good hunter will only take a safe shot. A good hunter will only take a shot that kills quickly so that the animal doesn't suffer.

The pitter patter of the gobbler is unmistakable. The leaves crinkle with each step. Minutes pass. Carlos slowly raises the gun. BANG! A perfect shot kills the bird. And for the first time in nearly an hour, I hear Carlos's voice. He is ecstatic. I am overcome.

As we survey the scene, I realize this will be one of the best days of the year—perhaps one of the better days of my life. Not because we killed a bird, but because I watched my son's passion bloom as he learned something new. And I was able to sit beside him as he undertook a challenge, used the knowledge he'd accumulated, and put it into practice. And, above all, that he was willing to share it with me. This was, for both me and Carlos, a perfect Daddy Day.

• • •

As I began writing *Daddy Days,* I asked each of my children—Maria, Carlos, and Cecilia—to share a reflection about the dedicated time we've spent together over many decades. I was struck by what Carlos shared about that hunting expedition we embarked on fifteen years ago:

> My dad was never the hunting type. But when I asked if I could get into it, his response was supportive. He took time out of his busy schedule to sign up for hunter's education and attend weekly classes for a month. He also agreed to bring me hunting with Dwayne one cold spring morning. It was such a memorable experience for me, with my dad by my side for all of it. He was always supportive and encouraging, even if it wasn't exactly his cup of tea. I may not have appreciated it fully at the time, but in hindsight this trip really showed my dad's unconditional love for me and willingness to participate happily and be interested in events

that were not his choice. Through his actions he passed on a great life skill that I work on to this day.

I should explain what a Daddy Day is. It's a simple formula: Each of my children receives a certificate at Christmas, a document that reminds them how much I love spending time with them and how proud I am of them. The certificate entitles them to a full day of one-on-one time (as you'll see, it's occasionally longer) in the coming year. They get to choose the place, the activity, the food. All of it. Your job as Dad is to just say "yes." If your kids are like mine, they will be smart about their choices and select activities that are reasonable, affordable, and fun. When he was ten, Carlos chose that day of turkey hunting.

My kids have requested treacherous hikes in the White Mountains, nervy sailing excursions in coastal waters, and sprawling Western adventures. The ultimate Daddy Days typically involve a serious adventure, as overcoming challenges together is one of the best ways I've found to strengthen the bond with my kids, a lesson I first learned by listening to Dr. Gary Smalley, a renowned counselor and founder of the Smalley Relationship Center. Smalley taught that families that overcome difficulties together ultimately grow closer—a concept that has been central to my family's experience.

In my effort to write this book, I started reflecting on the dozens of adventures I shared with my dad as well as the experiences I shared with my own kids. The overriding theme was that being intentional about sharing time together and engaging in difficult pursuits had helped me grow a strong relationship with each of my family members.

But this book was not only inspired by my family. It is also informed by countless conversations I've had with friends and acquaintances over the years, many of whom had broken relationships with their own dads and therefore struggled to maintain a healthy relationship with their children. According to the U.S. Census Bureau, one out of three children live without their biological dad in the home. Moreover, per the National

Fatherhood Initiative, having an involved father can reduce a child's risk for issues including emotional and behavioral problems, criminal activities, obesity, and suicide. In her own reflection, my oldest daughter, Maria, addressed this factor head on:

> In an age where kids struggle with anxiety and low self-esteem in record numbers, Daddy Days became more important than ever. I am convinced that a major source for my generally decent self-esteem was a healthy relationship with my dad. . . . As I have grown older, I have realized that Daddy Days were always special for reasons beyond the ability to do whatever I wanted. They were an opportunity every year to deepen my relationship with my dad—who was, and always will be—my hero. The consistency of a gift of time every year was a constant reminder that I was loved and that I mattered.

The person who first introduced the concept of Daddy Days, my own dad, was a giant in my eyes—my hero. I always wanted to spend time with him. I wanted to watch him fix his tractor with his bare hands in the winter. I wanted to work on projects with him, to hike mountains with him, and to ride on his boats even though they were barely seaworthy. He gave me the gift of time, and I've always tried to reinvest that gift in my own children. I'm not a perfect dad, but I've tried for thirty-two years to be a good father to my kids. I've tried for thirty-three years to be a good husband to my wife, Renée. And while I don't have it all figured out, I count it an enormous blessing that they are still willing to spend such dedicated time with me each year.

My dad was a great storyteller. I've thought for many years that I would just let my children tell the stories of Daddy Days, passing the concept on to their families, if not by practice at least by oral tradition. But this proverbial apple didn't fall far from the tree. Like my own dad, I like to tell stories, too, especially about my kids. This book is not just about sharing stories to keep memories alive. Over many decades, I've come to learn that being a father is one of the greatest gifts a man can receive and one of the most important jobs he will ever occupy. I've also learned countless lessons through time spent with my children, and I want to share them in hopes they will inspire fathers everywhere to deepen their relationships with their children.

The tales that follow about Daddy Days are not merely happy anecdotes; they weave together a story about the joys of fatherhood and the countless ways relationships can evolve between parents and their children. Like many of the stories in the pages that follow, this book is a journey, a winding trail on which we'll explore the blessings that come from being a dad. We are all somewhere in the journey of our relationship with our parents, children, and loved ones. While a solid relationship between a father and child undoubtedly requires more than one day each year, it is my hope that you will find useful stories and lessons in this book that help you grow closer to the people you love the most.

Required listening: *Prepare your heart for reading this book by listening to two songs: Harry Chapin's "Cat's in the Cradle" followed by Rodney Atkins's "Watching You." The songs present two very different models for fatherhood—one where a dad is present, and another where he is not. Reflect on which type of dad you want your children to remember and think about what you can do to fulfill Rodney Atkins's vision of fatherhood. Think of your children, perhaps your grandchildren, as your little buckaroos. Invest in them.*

PART 1

THE BIRTH OF DADDY DAYS

1 Being Present

My parents met in 1959 at a Halloween party in Haverhill, Massachusetts, where, as the story goes, my dad was workshopping a joke about there being dead shrimp in the party dip. I don't know what crustacean-oriented punchline he was setting up, or if he really executed it, but thankfully he found a warm—or perhaps forgiving—audience for his humor in my late mother, Joanne. My dad, Charles Francis Turner, had served in the Navy and was wrapping up his engineering degree. My mother was a Catholic high school teacher. Both were mature, hardworking, and ambitious. And both were ready to marry and get to business: Between 1961 and 1969, they had six kids. They were nothing if not efficient.

I always thought of my dad as a rock star. But not like Elvis or Michael Jackson. In fact, with my parents, there was only one radio station allowed in our home growing up: WCRB, which is Boston's classical radio station. If a radio was on in our house, it was tuned to this station playing Beethoven, Bach, Vivaldi, or some performance by the Boston Pops. Rock and roll (and pretty much every other music genre) was classified by my parents as inferior. We did have a record player, and I recall my older brother, C.J., brought home albums by Aerosmith and Steve Miller. When our parents were away for the night, we would jam to those records. While all my friends had color TVs, our home had no TV and just one radio.

Was I deprived? Hardly. Clearly, my parents understood that less noise and distraction in our home would help us read more books, explore the great outdoors, and enjoy our time spent with friends in our cul-de-sac Cricket Hill neighborhood in Amherst, New Hampshire (Renée and I bought the house from my dad after my mother passed in 2013). Our household was a bedrock of mindfulness.

My dad was never the strongest, funniest, smartest, or most handsome person in the room. But he's always been a solid, hard-working, God-fearing guy, liked by all who have known him. He was consistently kind, but not over the top. His tachometer just purrs at 2,000 rpm, nice and steady and with the longevity of a diesel engine—one that started purring in 1930 and is still tickin' today. He clearly understood why God gave us two ears and one mouth. He was a pleasant conversationalist, always giving you plenty of time to yap, but he would also enjoy sharing stories and asking probing questions. He was always delightfully present.

He was the stereotypical Yankee engineer. He knew how to do a great deal of things well. His project workmanship was not perfect, but it was pretty darn good. His workshop was always a little cluttered, but he prioritized important stuff in life: God, family, work, country. Ultimately, he was incredibly balanced. I recall him—for many years—strapping his briefcase and his cream cheese and olives on pumpernickel sandwich on the back of his ten-speed bike and then riding the ten miles or so each way to work at his desk job during the 1980s. He clearly understood that to be a good dad required that he stay fit and healthy. He was ahead of his time regarding work-life balance.

Growing up, I considered him very conservative. Classical music. Devout Catholic. Reagan Republican. Loyal husband. Drinking meant enjoying a glass of wine on Sunday—or perhaps a beer—but always in moderation. He was a careful spender, downright frugal by most standards. He was not the life of the party. Rather, he was the soul. He was even keeled, rarely angry, and I don't recall ever seeing him visibly upset with my mom (though I'm sure that there were times.) And while his politics and economic philosophy may have been conservative, his sense of adventure was cutting edge. He used to show photos of himself skiing

Tuckerman Ravine in the 1950s—along with a few very daring souls—way before parabolic-shaped skis and metal edges had been created.

When I was six, he had the idea of taking his city-girl wife and all five of us kids (aged four to twelve) on a weeklong backpacking and camping adventure to Isle au Haut, an island off Midcoast Maine accessible only by boat and with fewer than a hundred full-time residents. Isle au Haut is like the more popular Mount Desert Island (the home of Acadia National Park) minus the waiting lines on hiking trails, the traffic jams, the sunbathers on Sand Beach, and the throngs of cyclists and walkers on the carriage roads. When we first made the trip, it was in the days when the mailboat passenger ferry only stopped at the town of Isle au Haut and you had to hike five miles south to modest three-sided lean-tos.

We stayed there for a week. Hiking, blueberry picking, clamming, taking in sunsets from Eben's Head (heaven on earth, for the record) and trying to sleep with the mosquitoes biting our faces. We were at times wet, cold, hungry, and sore, but it was one of the best weeks of my life, honestly, and it grew into a full-throttle addiction to that island for most of us Turner kids.

My mom was amazing in her own right. She stepped up to the challenge with incredible organization and food management and meal production, planning non-perishable meals for us for a week. She cooked largely over the open campfire—and I'm sure that no one has as good a track record as her for consistently and perfectly cooking food in these conditions. She was a rock star, too. She produced food that remains among my favorites of all time: mashed potatoes (from dried flakes, of course) with Slim Jim slices mixed in (no joke, it is delicious), apples (from the wild apple trees nearby), dumplings (cooked over the campfire), and lentil soup.

My four siblings all agree that our family camping adventure trips to Isle au Haut were amazing. However, it's hard to share with your dad how you really feel about life and girls when your nosy sisters are listening, and your older brother is already years ahead of you into puberty. As my wife of thirty-two years reminds me often, a date has a very different feel when it's just the two of us versus attending a fundraising event with two hundred other people. Deep relationships are nourished by one-on-one conversations. My dad clearly recognized this, and while we continued to share family adventures, he saw an opportunity to create something else: a tool he called "Daddy Days."

I am not sure exactly when it began, but I recall getting certificates at Christmas for Daddy Days very early in my childhood. The basic principle of a Daddy Day was that the kid (the receiver) could pick an activity for a day with him and then his job was to make it real. Let's start with the roots of this idea: the era where my father showed his kids, quite literally, how it was done.

Lesson 1: Being Present. *Daddy Days are all about being fully present with ones we love—which is best achieved in one-on-one settings. Natural surroundings often facilitate mindfulness and the ability to share more of yourself. So, if you're trying to grow closer to your kids, think about how you're going to prepare your mind and heart for a real relationship. How will you unlock your best? Will it be over a campfire? A long drive? The core ingredient is time, the more the better. For most of us, we need lots of time to enjoy ourselves and to be in the right mood for serious conversations. Deep and personal relationships with our children are something we should all seek, but sometimes they require slowing down and being mindful above all else.*

Gratitude

One of my first Daddy Days was a trip to the New England Aquarium with my father. I was born in 1967, so it makes sense that he would have wanted to see the aquarium shortly after its opening in Boston in 1969. This is just part of the genius of Daddy Days. If you play your cards right, it's not just about what your kiddos want. It's about creatively spent days where the kid "picks" the adventure, but the dad gets to influence the activity. As I recall, the aquarium was perhaps my first Daddy Day at age four or five. Before long, our dedicated time together skewed toward more adventurous pursuits.

I was number four of the five living Turner children (my older brother Stephen died of sudden infant death syndrome). Siblings two and three are my sisters Mary and Sue, respectively. After a year or two of solo Daddy Days, we started scheming with Dad that perhaps we could bundle our days and create multiday "Dad-ventures." He was a great sport and thought that this was a brilliant idea, so we started planning adventures like climbing Mount Washington and staying at the Lake of the Clouds Hut. I'm not sure that we got our "full money's worth" (I think many of these were just one overnight) but enjoying the hut as a ten-year-old was a hoot. I recall card games with a bunch of big kids (they were probably mostly mid-teens) and typical hikers: inclusive, team players, but pleasantly competitive.

This became a pattern for Sue, Mary, and me. In 1978, we backpacked into the Pemigewasset Wilderness, set up a camp along the East Branch of the Pemigewasset River, did an overnight, then day-hiked a loop in the wilderness, did a "cold plunge" in the river, enjoying a second night in the same spot before concluding with a hike up and over Mount Carrigan. My dad injured himself on the second day, but a kind and macho forest ranger carried some of Dad's gear up and over the mountain. I long remembered the strength of that ranger, who carried fresh apples to add some weight to his pack. Despite that injury, it was such a stirring adventure that I repeated it about twenty years later with my own young family and one of our favorite tagalongs, my nephew James Clague. The ultimate place to view stars in New Hampshire is from the rocks in the middle of the east branch of the Pemigewasset River, about as removed from light pollution as any place in the Granite State.

My most memorable Daddy Day as a kid came in 1979, when I was twelve. My dad arranged for a float plane to deliver the four of us onto a remote pond east of the Turner Mountains in Baxter State Park, Maine, near Mount Katahdin. One of my dad's ancestors, Charles Turner Jr., was a surveyor from Massachusetts who made the first documented ascent of Katahdin in 1804. It was for this Turner that the three peaks—North, South, and East Turner Mountain—were named. Naturally my dad wanted to explore the area—and why not bring his kiddos along? We thought this idea was genius.

The plane was so small that my sister Mary and I were delivered first and then my dad and Sue followed about an hour later. No communication devices. No guns. No trail. No sun. No GPS. No bear spray. No backup plans. We then began a wet two-day bushwhack back to civilization. For most hikers, it's considered an achievement to hike Mount Katahdin and the Knife Edge trail following worn, easy-to-follow paths. My 2019 Baxter State Park Trail map shows a trail from Katahdin Lake to Twin Ponds, but I'm sure that we were not following a trail in the 1970s.

We fought through brush and forest, blazing our own trail. We climbed trees to observe progress and used a compass to find our way around the east side of East Turner Mountain. We made it to Twin Ponds for our first wilderness night and set up a campsite. I'm pretty sure we carried no flashlight, and we had limited food and relatively lame gear by modern standards. We were wet and cold, but we arose the next morning and found our way up the uncharted east side of South Turner Mountain. In hindsight, this adventure was as scary as it was exhilarating, and yet somehow, with my dad, things always felt in control. He was calm, which made these adventures feel uncommonly safe.

Whether it was bushwhacking through the wilderness or piloting overloaded lake boats across Penobscot Bay, my dad's brave spirit reminded me a little of the 1961 film *El Cid*, where a Spanish protagonist fights for what is right and true. My favorite version stars Charlton Heston and Sophia Loren. El Cid was a man of incredible integrity and bravery, so much so that Spaniards flocked to follow him into battle. In the movie's final scene, to inspire his army, his wife has his dead body mounted on his loyal steed to lead his followers to fight the Moors on the beaches of Valencia. In a less dramatic way, my dad's integrity and bravery inspired us to follow him on all kinds of adventures.

My dad had incredible energy—and not just physically. He had energy you could *feel* when he walked in the room. He exuded an air of peaceful gratitude. He was not a generous tipper with money—he didn't have it to give. But he was generous in the way he offered thanks to those around him. He would take the time to get to know names of those serving and helping him, with a calm but positive demeanor conveying how grateful he really was. It was infectious. In some ways, he was a people whisperer, with a spirit that drew people to him. Throughout our Daddy Days adventures, I learned the importance of gratitude by watching the way he interacted with the world.

The Daddy Days of my early childhood were largely intense physical adventures with backpacking being the most common form of recreation. It was wonderful to share these times with my sisters, and I credit the strong relationship we have today to some of those early adventures. In the years to come, though, my dad and I would spend more one-on-one time together working on projects beyond my imagination—and my gratitude for that time would be immeasurable.

Lesson 2: Gratitude. *I will forever be grateful that my dad took time every year to give me the gift of Daddy Days when I was young. It was only one day each year—at least formally—but the joy and anticipation would linger all year long. When you give or receive the promise of a Daddy Day, you might spend six months or more just thinking about how you will spend this time. You can spend another six months looking at the pictures of the activity, reminiscing about how much fun it was and thinking about what next year's Daddy Day might consist of. As you plan one-on-one time with your children, remember that they are always watching the way you interact with those around you. If you model gratitude for them, they will likely remain grateful for your time the rest of their lives.*

Perseverance

One of the greatest memories from my childhood was actually a day I spent with my mom. By 1981, our family was hooked on our annual family vacations at Isle au Haut. At this point, we had been visiting every summer for at least seven years. We began renting a house in Rich's Cove from a universally adored woman we knew as Miss Lizzie. The island postmistress for decades, she was such an icon on the island that they eventually named a passenger ferry after her. I was a freshman in high school and Dad had limited vacation time. So, when my folks learned of a house for sale on Isle au Haut, my mom took me out of school and headed up to check out our very-distant relatives Harold and Elthea Turner's house, which was for sale. I recall the jovial realtor, Don Lord, suggesting that the east (water-facing) side of this house was crying for a deck. I agreed.

It was a March day, and relatively pleasant given the season. I explored the thirteen-acre property while Mom looked at the house. Exploring buildings and woods are two of my greatest pleasures in life, and I did both that critical day. I snapped photos with my yard-sale-bought 35mm camera before my mom and I took the mailboat to the mainland and reported back to my dad (by pay phone, of course) what we found. I implored him to proceed with the purchase. I'm sure that I told him about the collapsed barn roof and the absence of running water, but the thought of my family owning a piece of Isle au Haut was simply magical for me at fourteen years old. I surely had no idea how much work was ahead to turn this property into the summer-rental operation my parents were envisioning so they could afford it on a modest income.

Looking back, this day was a telling example of the faith and courage my dad had in me. I love my kids, but I cannot imagine trusting any of them at fourteen years old to evaluate a property purchase for me. It was my first real home inspection—one that ultimately led me to a career in the building inspection and engineering business. My dad's trust in me instilled incredible confidence, a lesson that I carry with me today.

• • •

The property was already called Turner Cove. My dad owned a seventeen-foot aluminum lake fishing boat named *Lucky Ducky* at the time, which became our primary construction material transport. Nearly every crossing involved large and heavy building material—which in that boat made for a wet experience. For those unfamiliar with boating in the Gulf of Maine, the natural state of affairs—especially when you are riding in the wrong vessel—involves being soaked by 50-degree ocean water. Any chop results in spray coming over the bow. When you arrive an hour later to your destination, you're frozen, or "colder than a well-driller's butt" as they say up there. My dad, being a Yankee on a modest income, did not invest much in foul weather gear for those voyages.

The regular trips to Isle au Haut—through the remainder of my high school days—became my later Daddy Days. It was always an adventure, with plenty of work thrown in. There is a simple reason that island property is generally worth 50 percent of the value of mainland property. The logistics of island life are complex. For instance, you buy two-by-fours at your local lumberyard during the week prior to the trip. You load them in your truck. Perhaps you unload them at your home and reload them when you are preparing to leave for the trip to Maine. Then you unload them from your truck and haul them down to your boat, and if your luck is like ours consistently was, you are loading and unloading the boat at low tide—adding an extra ten to fifteen feet of vertical drop to the effort.

Assuming you survive the crossing, you now unload the two-by-fours from your boat onto the dinghy and then from the dinghy to the shore and carry them up to the barn or garage to store them. You handle everything at least five times more than you would on the mainland, where construction materials typically go directly from the store to the worksite. We always concluded, however, that work at Isle au Haut was worth it because the jobs treated you to a million-dollar view looking northeast across Jericho Bay to Mount Desert Island.

Oh, and the deal got even sweeter. There were neither showers nor toilets when we bought the property. Instead, we had an in-house "outhouse" in the basement, a big metal bucket under a wood box, a.k.a. the toilet seat cover; the bucket needed to be dumped daily. My job was to dump the "honey" bucket. My occasional reward came in the form of beautiful young women who would come to explore the island, like the three Methvin daughters. Eugene Methvin was a *Reader's Digest* senior editor who brought his three daughters to Turner Cove. This guy was a character, singing each morning as he strutted down to the waterfront for his swim. Later in the day, his daughters would sunbathe on the lawn while I "worked" on the barn. The view working at Turner Cove was better than ever.

Still, the perennial adventure on all these trips to Isle au Haut remained the boat rides. Early on, my dad decided to build his own septic tank—essentially a four-by-eight-by-four-foot box made of plywood, wrapped in fiberglass, not unlike a boat. It barely fit when we placed it in his seventeen-foot boat. I rode out with him—the two of us in front of the box—motor behind the box, praying that nothing caused the boat to capsize or the motor to fail. We survived, and it was one of many small triumphs that allowed our dream on the island to take shape.

My dad's tolerance for pain and risk did know at least *some* limits. After a year or two of wet crossings in *Lucky Ducky*, my parents put in the winning bid for a boat that had been recovered in a drug bust—an eighteen-foot Squadron Yacht launch-style craft with a 14-hp diesel engine. This boat was safer, and it would keep us drier, but it was excruciatingly slow. *L'Esprit*, as she was called, had a maximum cruising speed of six knots and a finicky throttle that automatically settled back to about 1500 rpm, good for about 4.5 knots of boat speed. Now, I'm a sailor, and cruising at six knots with the wind in your sails and a gunwale buried in the water is thrilling. Somehow, motorboats just feel downright pokey at less than twenty knots. Despite her lack of speed, the bright red *L'Esprit* was something to behold. She even ended up in the pages of an L.L.Bean catalog one year.

My dad. Inventor of Daddy Days. Seated at center with my amazing mom. Both surrounded by their five children and lots of the grandchildren, with *L'Esprit* in the background on Isle au Haut.

• • •

I love boat names. When I stroll through a marina or boat yard, I don't just look at the various hull designs; I study the names. Stonington, Maine, is the lobster capital of the world, and with a fleet of over three hundred boats, there are myriad names to contemplate. One of my all-time favorites is *Perseverance*. It is exactly what successful lobstermen do. In my opinion, their job is right up there with steel erection in terms of requiring guts. Naturally, it's also a great description of my dad's commitment to owning and improving Turner Cove. Now that I'm nearly sixty, I often reflect in admiration on how my dad started this adventure at age fifty-one. We worked hard. We still work hard. It was only a couple summers ago that I helped put yet another new roof on the barn. My dad taught me the perseverance and determination to set and complete goals through our many renovation projects at Turner Cove.

We made countless trips to Isle au Haut together. Many of these were just my dad and me driving five to six hours each way in his truck, schlepping materials onto the boat, and then slowly crossing the bay on *L'Esprit*, giving us ample time for conversation and prayer (in some cases, asking God to keep us afloat). I am glad we got to experience all those crossings together, and I am also grateful that *L'Esprit* was so slow. My dad would listen to me. My dreams. My ideas. My questions. As my wonderful wife Renée often reminds me, you show someone that you love them by spending one-on-one time with them. My dad gave me that one-on-one time at Isle au Haut as I advanced through high school and college, and it's a lesson I would never forget.

My dad had pretty much dropped the formal "Daddy Day" concept once Turner Cove entered our lives. I'm certainly not complaining. Turner Cove became an inspiring family connection, one that was important to keep my siblings united. Plus, many of my own children's fond memories can be traced to Isle au Haut visits—my first grandchild even made his first visit recently. And none of it would have been possible without my mom's and dad's perseverance.

Lesson 3: Perseverance. *I don't think my dad had it all pre-planned, but his ownership of a fixer-upper house on Isle au Haut gave us lots of one-on-one time. Long trips, long boat rides, long hikes, and labor-intensive projects all offered time for conversation. And watching him stay focused, work hard, and overcome obstacles instilled in me a work ethic for which I remain grateful today. Think about this in your own life. As you make plans with your children, are you giving them an opportunity to watch you persevere through something challenging? Are you achieving something difficult together? Set big goals and work with your children to accomplish them.*

Transitions

In 1986, I was off to the University of Maine, Orono. Of course, I wanted to be close to Isle au Haut, which was probably not a fantastic reason to select a college but it satisfied my thirst for independence. It was a little farther away from home than the University of New Hampshire, and I figured that would be good for me. This was long before email, text, and unlimited free calling. My dad sent me at least one letter every week when I was in college, an incredible correspondence that became a highlight of my college days. We still managed many long-weekend visits to Isle au Haut, and I recall my parents allowing me to bring my Malaysian friend and fellow engineering student, Elango, home for Thanksgiving and to the island one year.

I powered my way through engineering school in three and a half years, figuring that life would be more fun with a good salary instead of accumulating debt. I scored a job with Texas Instruments in their sales training program. After one year in Houston and another in Dallas, I missed New England too much, particularly the outdoor adventures, Isle au Haut, and my family. So, I requested a transfer to the Waltham, Massachusetts, sales office. When I got the job, I became the only Texas Instruments sales trainee with the license plate reading: *BUY TI.* The company was paying me a great salary, so I figured why not show a little love?

In 1991, while working and living in Massachusetts, I finally met Renée. She was beautiful, intelligent and shared my Catholic faith. She was a Cuban immigrant, raised in New York and Texas, and was studying at Boston University. She was small in stature but big in personality—a true pistol. Her dad died when she was only twenty-one, but she tells me that he was a kind and joyful father. Before long we were married and got to work on that six-kid family we both dreamed of.

In 1994, we were blessed with our first, Maria Felicita. We miscarried little Joey two years later and never conceived again. Not everyone in this world is blessed with the gift of fertility. We decided that we would try to adopt and were subsequently blessed to welcome Carlos and Cecilia into our life, both of whom came from Romania. Our family was now really taking shape.

In the early years of our marriage, Renée was still working on her dissertation for her doctorate, and it took me too long to figure out that the only way my wife was going to finish was if I took Maria away on adventures. So, even before she could understand Daddy Days, I was taking Maria on father-daughter hikes and beach adventures. One of those more memorable adventures was up Mount Chocorua in the White Mountains of New Hampshire when she was only three. I recall her climbing about half of it and riding on my shoulders for the other half. I may not have known it as she rode on my shoulders, but a tradition would soon reemerge.

Lesson 4: Transitions. *The journalist Bob Phillips is credited with saying: "There are three stages of a man: He believes in Santa Claus, he does not believe in Santa Claus, he is Santa Claus." Making transitions from adolescence to adulthood to married life and eventually fatherhood—becoming Santa Claus—is a foundational step on the way to becoming a good father. In these years, it's important to maintain a strong relationship with your parents, if you still have them, and find someone with whom you can build a strong foundation. And enjoy the one-on-one time you have with your spouse. Use that time to become a man who is ready for fatherhood.*

PART 2

THE SECOND GENERATION

Purposefulness

By the time Maria was four, I made it official. It was time to continue the Daddy Day tradition with my family. She recently located her first certificate—which she redeemed for a day at the Boston Children's Museum. While we had a lovely time at the museum, I had not at that point mastered the combination of adventure and bonding my dad could so deftly inspire. While mentally stimulating, the museum was a relatively low-risk endeavor. Fortunately, as our relationship evolved, so would our activities.

Among the more memorable Daddy Days Maria and I shared when she was young was a trip to Plymouth Plantation (now called Plimoth Patuxet Museums). It was a day full of history lessons in which Maria was inspired by, of all things, gardening and weeding. In the years to follow, she would become a determined weeder at our home—not something I expected to happen, but a welcome lesson nonetheless. But this also marked our first father-daughter camping expedition. When we retreated to our campground for the night, we discovered that I'd forgotten something critically important, as Maria remembers:

> I was eight years old and had a desire to see Plymouth Plantation, probably thanks to a good history lesson in school. I remember learning from an actor on the model *Mayflower* about the distinction between the "English" and the "British." I remember watching in fascination as a Native American carved a canoe out of

a log. Perhaps most shocking was the enthusiasm I had for helping Martha Brown weed her vegetable garden. The camping was memorable too. My dad forgot the tent, so we slept in a makeshift lean-to he made out of the tarp he had brought.

Despite my oversight, Maria became hooked on camping and a variety of outdoor pursuits. Maria was probably eleven years old when we first tackled Mount Washington, which at 6,288 feet is the most prominent peak east of the Mississippi River and a rite of passage for any New England hiker. Maria and I climbed the Ammonoosuc Ravine Trail, stayed overnight at the AMC Lake of the Clouds hut, and then summited Mount Washington and climbed down. It was a formative moment for us, as Maria noted in her reflection for this book:

> After summiting Mount Washington, most of my Daddy Days from that point on were hikes. Our days have been spent hiking all over New Hampshire, Maine, and Vermont. My dad and I decided we wanted to tackle the New Hampshire Four-thousand Footers list. This occupied us for a few years. After finishing the 48, we started working on the Vermont Long Trail, a 273-mile hike across the Green Mountains. We would hike in sections, doing an overnight in order to knock out fifteen to twenty miles at a time. Our progress was interrupted by the birth of my son, but we plan to slowly knock out the miles of this continuous hike in the years to come.

In 2014, Maria and I planned an adventure that was designed to cross a batch of Four-thousand Footers off our list. We took on half the Pemi Loop, which surrounds the Pemigewasset Wilderness and is one of the most rugged hiking routes in the northeast. In fact, it's considered the second-hardest day-hike in America, though most people break it up into several days as we did in early October. We parked at the Gale River

Maria summits Washington for the first time.

Loop, summited Mount Garfield in 50-degree weather, then tackled the nearby Mount Galehead. From there, we took on the North and South Twin Mountain peaks and Mount Guyot, and set up our tent on a platform at Guyot Campsite. We awoke the next morning to eight inches of fresh powder. The views into the Pemigewasset Wilderness from Mount Bond, West Bond, and Bond Cliff were among the best I've ever seen. A rainbow of color unfolded with white snow above thirty-five hundred feet, then green conifers and orange, yellow, and red maples painting the valley below. This was one of the most glorious moments we shared on a trail together.

But when it came to planning hikes, Maria probably trusted me more than she should have. Most people who have backpacked with me would agree that I have horrible luck (or, rather, foresight) when it comes to weather. One example was a more recent Daddy Day with Maria when we decided to tackle the Percy Peaks—twin three-thousand-foot bald peaks near Stark, New Hampshire (and two mountains on another list, the 52 with a view)—during a one-hundred-year rain event. In classic John Turner form, I'd not carefully checked the weather *or* the maps. Before long, the trail was no longer really a path through the woods. Underfoot was a steady stream of water, which sloshed in and out of my ankle-high boots with every step. Torrents of rain pelted my jacket and ran down my legs. There was no way to avoid getting soaked.

Even worse, I did not have a good handle on the trail, so we sloshed all the way to Christine Lake, at least three or four times farther than we'd anticipated hiking. I was frustrated with myself for such an egregious navigational error, and we dropped our packs on the shoreline and stomped our way fully clothed into the comparatively warm lake water for a "cooldown" swim.

Somehow, we kept slogging. We still had a grand time, summiting South Percy that day despite being thoroughly soaked. We tackled the second peak early the next day, hiked out, and then hit Mass and the laundromat in Northumberland to dry our gear before heading to our second destination, the Cohos Trail near Dixville Notch. We bought new hiking boots for Maria in Colebrook (because sometimes Daddy Days mean splurging a little). And in Dixville, among other things, we explored the old Balsams hotel and were reprimanded by security. I was able to cool the situation down when I suggested I was simply seeking a great venue for my daughter's wedding. Early that evening, we began hiking back into the woods and at dusk, we set up camp next to a rushing stream on the Table Rock trail. We fell asleep listening to nature's lullabies.

I'm proud to say that I've hiked more mountains with Maria than anyone else. Often, it would just be the two of us backpacking for single overnights. She is one of the toughest athletes I know, and with a personality that matches her middle name (Felicita, meaning "happy"), she rarely complains. You never know where you'll build a relationship with your children, but for Maria and me, it was so often on the granite trails of northern New Hampshire. Our hikes were physically strenuous,

Soaking-wet summit smiles on South Percy Peak.

yes, but more importantly they offered a God-given venue to learn more about each other. With each bootstep, we would dive into our lives, our dreams, our worries, and our hopes. Just take it from Maria:

> Conversations can twist and turn covering a wide range of topics from a story about a student of mine, to a book I'm reading, to politics. In the course of my Daddy Days I have learned about my dad's childhood, his business, and during a recent one he told me about his goal to write this book. A huge part of a relationship is a constant sharing of self, and Daddy Days provide a wonderful opportunity to deeply reconnect and share. . . . Due to their annual nature, Daddy Days have become a chance to measure and mark important life events. I vividly remember talking to my dad about this guy I had met in grad school as we hiked up to the peak at Dixville Notch. That guy would become my husband two years later.

I will never forget that crazy rainy Percy adventure when Maria first told me about a man from Bedford, New Hampshire, who was in her master's program at Providence College. It's not that I wouldn't have learned about John Philip Schappler (same first and middle name as mine) any other way, but that Daddy Day happened to fall at a good time for us to have the conversation.

Lesson 5: Purposefulness. *With every Daddy Day I spend with my kids, there is a purpose behind it. Obviously, one objective is to have fun. A second is creating a safe space for deep and intimate conversation. If you create a safe space for your child from a young age, they will share their dreams and fears with you. Let them share. Encourage them. Remind them how loved they are. Remind them that you will love them no matter the course they set. This doesn't have to happen on a hiking trail, but it's essential to find the space for purposeful conversation.*

Listening

Recently, I spoke with Cecilia about my effort to write this book. She suggested that one of her earliest and most fond Daddy Day memories included eating bright blue ice cream in Marblehead, Massachusetts. She mentioned that I was somehow holding her upside down while she painted her tongue with the treat. This was probably around 2005.

It occurs to me now that Marblehead was an example of me being a bit selfish. I *love* sailboats and beaches, so by taking my daughter to this extraordinary harbor, I was able to enjoy both the sights and the company of my kiddo—and she was able to enjoy the beach and some blue ice cream. Win-win, right? This strategy seemed to work well when she was four years old, but things change. As kids grow, it's essential to listen

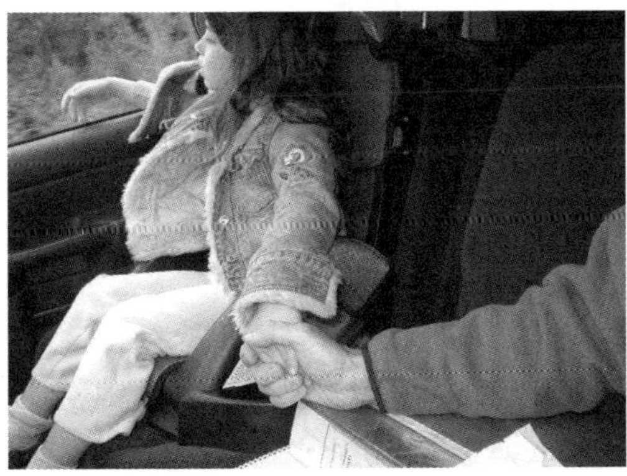

On a Daddy Day, Cecilia enjoys the hand and seat normally reserved for her mother.

to *their* passions and let that guide your activities. Cecilia described that evolution well when I asked her about it:

> Being the youngest I always watched my older siblings, my cousins, and mom receive experiences with my dad that I hadn't. Eventually this led to some slight jealousy. I was so excited when I received my first Daddy Day certificate, but I'm not sure exactly at what point I actually started to choose the activities we went on. As I grew up, my interests changed from amusement parks to shopping and getting my ears pierced. I dragged my dad on shopping trip after shopping trip when I became a tween.

Cecilia at Storyland—ever the ride-loving amusement park fun-companion.

Cecilia can be a princess. When she was young, if I said black, she would say white, and brainstorming Daddy Days with her took me out of my comfort zone. She was probably in middle school when she wanted a second ear piercing. Renée, my Cuban bride, seemed to think every girl should get their ears pierced as an infant so that they can quickly don gold studs. Multiple piercings, though, is not tradition and thus not approved. Daddy Days, however, provide opportunities to mix things up.

That year, Cecilia asked to go shopping in Massachusetts and have lunch at the Cheesecake Factory. In a somewhat clandestine affair, Cecilia and I also ended up at a mall-based ear-piercing shop. I know, it's probably no big deal for many, but it really was one of those fun little bonding moments for Cecilia and me. It still stands out as an example of Daddy Day magic because it was an early example of Cecilia deciding for herself. I figured another ear piercing was pretty low risk. Worst case, if Cecilia changed her mind (or if her mom vetoed the new piercing), it would quickly heal. But for me, it was an important opportunity to let my daughter experience the joy—or pain—of making her own choices.

Cecilia—at seven—already demonstrating some attitude.

To this day, Cecilia and I have a strong relationship. She knows that I'll support her in any decision that will not permanently negatively affect her. A more recent example of this was when I cosigned her loan for a

Jeep. At the time she still had student loans, and I would have greatly preferred that she purchase a less expensive vehicle. But I supported her because I knew that this was only a financial move, and children thrive when we support them in making choices. Of course, parents must be careful not to let their kids do something that could have irrevocable negative impacts, but in this instance, I trusted my daughter.

While Cecilia and I have many different interests, we do share a love of the water. One of my most cherished memories with her came in 2018, when for a Daddy Day we drove to Six Flags in Agawam, Massachusetts, enjoying a morning of high-thrill rides. It was a blistering hot day and the lines at the Six Flags water park in the afternoon were lengthy, so we passed on cooling off. Instead, I took my preferred route back—up Interstate 91 to Brattleboro, Vermont—and then 101 East through Keene, New Hampshire, which put us at Dublin Lake about 6 P.M.

Dublin Lake is spectacular—it's a classic clean and clear New Hampshire cold lake (the warm lakes have a more brownish tinge). There are a number of vehicle turn-outs along this section where it appears to be public land, so you can simply park, climb down a few rocks to the water's edge, and jump in. When you surface, you admire the entire west slope of Grand Monadnock, one of the most climbed mountains in the world. On a summer evening, the water temperature is perfect—cool enough that it's refreshing, warm enough that you don't feel like you are doing a polar plunge. While we both love water, Cecilia is a much better swimmer. So, we hung out for a while in the water, admiring the mountain and watching the low and late sun make its way to the horizon. We talked about life, her dreams, and—probably—what flavor ice cream we'd pick up on the way home. For me, it was one of those moments that reminded me how much I love New Hampshire and how delighted I was to share the natural world with my daughter. Cecilia later told me jumping in the lake was her favorite part of the day. My kind of girl.

In March 2020, Cecilia had asked me to go to a cake-decorating school in Boston with her. Now, to be clear, my idea of a good time on a cold day in March is to put on my Levi's, my Chippewa logger boots, and my chaps, and fire up my Husqvarna chainsaw to drop an eighty-foot red oak. But Daddy Days are a promise. So, off we went to this (no surprise) all-female event. The class was all about how to decorate cakes—and it occurred just prior to Saint Patrick's Day in Boston—so we were armed with green frosting, shamrocks, and good cheer.

Cake decorating class in Boston together.

Spending time together—doing something fun—is a great way to break the ice. You don't talk about sensitive issues while you are with a group decorating cupcakes, but it helps you relax and facilitates a serious heart-to-heart conversation afterwards. We followed it with lunch, naturally, at the Cheesecake Factory, which was nearly abandoned that day as Covid-19 protocols were taking hold. We were both grateful that we fit her 2020 Daddy Day in just before the pandemic locked down the world.

Ear piercings and baking classes may not have topped my list of activities, but those things mattered to Cecilia. And that's the point of Daddy Days—it's about what your kid wants to do. And while it can be challenging, there are unexpected memories you'll make with your kids if you're willing to put your own agenda aside and listen.

• • •

Carlos continues to teach me this lesson each year. When I was young, I loved Tonka trucks. I had a classic dump truck and payloader, and I envied the kids who had excavators. So, when Carlos was three, I built a beautiful sandbox for him and purchased some Tonkas. Silly me. Tonkas were simply not his thing. For Carlos, it was G.I. Joes and plastic soldiers. He would create armies fighting between one side of his bedroom and another. I still don't understand the attraction, but it's a reminder that we are only partially a product of our environment; we are also born with natural inspiration and inclination. Somehow, soldiers and guns inspired Carlos. It was hard, and I was not particularly inspired to play war games, but I was trying to understand my son's interests.

Go karts with Carlos was probably more my influence—but he was always a great sport about our early Daddy Day activities.

Enter Daddy Days. Six Gun City in Jefferson, New Hampshire, (sadly, it's now closed) was an adorable little Western theme park. Freedom is one of the few New Hampshire towns with a Western Big Sky feel (its proximity to the Presidential Mountain Range certainly helps). Six Gun City had the dusty dirt main street with all the attractions you would expect: saloon, bank, trading post, and more. You could go searching for gold in the "stream" or shoot up the town (the concept would never fly today). So, for a Daddy Day when he was four years old, we made the trip. Carlos and I enjoyed the cowboy chaos and the associated water park. We'd return a number of times over the years, and before long we'd become regulars at the Lantern Inn Campground (now the Lantern "Resort"). Back when we were regular visitors to this establishment, the Lantern Inn piped music into their swimming pool (yes, below the water), and I would stay under there as long as possible grooving to Michael Jackson.

The boys are ready to go shoot up the town at Six Gun City.

Those trips to Six Gun City were just a precursor to Carlos's budding interest in hunting. I recall one Sunday morning in 2008 on our way home from church, he and I discovered a fresh raccoon roadkill on Mill's Hill in Dunbarton. We stopped, scooped up the poor critter, and gave him a ride home in the back of the pickup. At home, I challenged Carlos to gut him, salvage the pelt, and dispose of the remainder respectfully. Maria helped.

I gagged. To Carlos's credit, that skin hung in our mudroom for over a decade. It was a great memory of Carlos's interest in hunting.

As Carlos's harvesting skills grew, some of our best Daddy Days together were hunting based. My respect for hunters and hunting grew, and I of course enjoyed the outdoor adventures. But to share those memories together, I had to let go of my priorities for Carlos and let him show me his passion.

Lesson 6: Listen to your kids! *I've had to adapt to activities that wouldn't have been on my top ten list. And you know what? It was all good every time. We grow when we try new things. Putting a smile on their face and on your heart is essential emotional exercise—and it sure helps remind the giftees that you really do love them. There will always be an opportunity to teach your kids something that you love, to share your passions with them. But sometimes, you need to let them show you what they're most interested in. Your job is to lean in and try to understand them better.*

7 Delayed Gratification

The jovial old man Harold Turner, former owner of Turner Cove, had a funny saying that the wind in Burnt Island Thorofare (northeast corner of Isle au Haut) would "blow the hair off a dog." This was one of those days. It was January 2015 and the surf was crashing and the wind was whipping up the sea as we clambered over rocks at the tip of Trial Point. It was cold, but the views west to Vinalhaven and Camden Hills were second to none. Fortunately, skies were clear and the sun was warm, especially when we were in more protected zones like the inner harbor at Seal Trap. Maria and I were on a mission, and when you keep moving in cold conditions, you keep warm. Conditions on that cold winter day were also favorable as the ground was generally clear of snow and ice, so footing on the rocky shores was stable. This was part of a multiyear Daddy-Day mission. Our motivation was high.

Most ideas that lead to Daddy Days are not dreamt up in any given moment; rather, they develop over time. For instance, after all our years spent on Isle au Haut, Maria proposed that we circumnavigate-hike the coastline of Isle au Haut. Now, you may think this is no brave undertaking, as the island is only three miles wide by six miles long. And if it were a rectangle, the perimeter would be only eighteen miles. Good runners would knock that out in three hours, it's true. But the coastline is more like twenty-five miles around. That's still less than a marathon that many people crank out in four hours. But what if the "rule" of this adventure was that you could only pass between the trees and the waterline? It would be an easy rule to follow if jogging on a beach, but this is Penobscot Bay, Maine, where the coastline varies. Dead spruce trees line edges of the island, and cliffs and rock outcroppings govern other sections of the would-be trail.

We started this adventure when Maria was a teenager, knocking out stretches as part of various summertime visits to the island, clambering up and down the craggy shoreline whenever we could find a few hours of free time. We were about halfway around the island one year when we decided to make the remainder a Daddy Day. My sister, Sue, and her husband, Stewart (now owners of Turner Cove), graciously let us make the winter visit—which we did one year over the New Year's weekend. Having a warm place to sleep at night meant we'd have running water for toilets and cooking—very welcome after intense hikes. We were granted a glorious weekend: bright sun, blue skies, and very cold.

Maria and I both enjoyed how this adventure was spaced out over the years, picking up where we left off each time. It was not a premeditated goal to strengthen our patience and willpower for delayed gratification, but reflecting on it now, that's precisely what it was. Not everything in life comes easily—and lots of things require patience and delayed gratification. Some adventures, like completing the Four-thousand Footers list or circumnavigating Isle au Haut, should not be a race. Rather, the goal itself becomes rhythm, like a metronome that steadily beats as the years go by. It took Maria and me about fifteen years to finish the Four-thousand Footers together. It took us several years of day hikes to make it all the way around the island.

Spreading memories out over time has remained a pattern with Maria's more recent Daddy Days. I'm fortunate that her husband, John, has allowed me to continue enjoying these adventures with her. About five years ago, we started hiking the Long Trail in Vermont and so far have completed three legs. We started in North Adams, Massachusetts, and did one overnight on Consultation Peak, returning to our car at Route 9. The next year we tackled Route 9 to the Stratton-Arlington Road. In

Completion of our shore hike around the perimeter of Isle au Haut.

year three we made it to Bromley. Then Maria got pregnant, so our last two Daddy Days have been more moderate hikes with her little cherub, Andrew. Rumor has it that soon we'll be back on the Long Trail together. I want to finish the Long Trail with her, and there will be a tremendous amount of delayed gratification when I do.

The concept of delayed gratification has now been built into my side business and number one hobby: Christmas tree farming. About fifteen years ago, Renée inspired me to satisfy an urge to become a farmer by going to the New Hampshire State Farm and Garden show. It was the spring of 2011 and we met Jeff Taylor and his lovely bride, Sue, of Windswept Mountain View Christmas Tree Farm in Richmond, New Hampshire. It did not take long before Jeff convinced me that I had all of the skills necessary—and the right property—to become a Christmas tree farmer.

Renée had agreed that we could sell our beautiful home in Dunbarton, which we called Casa Del Sol, and purchase an agricultural property.

In the thick of our decision process, my mother passed away and Dad was willing to sell us his ten-acre hilltop property in Amherst—the perfect place for a cut-your-own Christmas tree farm. A few years into clearing our woodlot and planting baby Christmas trees, our son Carlos suggested that we should call it "Live Tree or Die Farm"—a fun play on the New Hampshire state motto General John Stark gave us: Live Free or Die.

The average time from planting a Christmas tree to harvest is typically eight to nine years. Every year, you mulch, fertilize, weed, prune, and shear each tree. If the deer don't eat them, the drought doesn't kill them, the mice don't eat their bark, and the root fungus doesn't attack them from below, then you might end up with a tree you can sell. It is the ultimate test of patience. But I don't regret it for a moment, because there are few more joyful noises in life than hearing children squeal with delight as they decide which beautiful evergreen will sit in their living room.

Lesson 7: Delayed Gratification. *The best things in life take time. Setting goals with your kids—milestones that can be achieved over years, not days—is an excellent way to grow closer. By the time you finally accomplish that goal, both you and your child will realize you helped each other to the finish line. Delayed gratification also builds patience, an essential ingredient in any loving relationship. Bookmark Corinthians Chapter 13 and always remember: "Love is patient and kind."*

8 Flexibility

Things were not looking good. We'd been hunting for days, and while Carlos and I had spent precious time together, at our current trajectory we would not be bringing elk steaks home from Montana. My brother wanted us to see his latest construction project—a new house on a multi-hundred-acre ranch. As we drove in on the mile-plus private driveway, my brother emphatically told us that we were *not* permitted to hunt on this land. So, naturally as we toured the nearly completed house in the late afternoon, two deer were grazing in the backyard. The owner knew why Carlos and I had come to Montana and asked Carlos if he had his gun with him. The kind owner said: "Go get it and have some fun!" Without hesitation, Carlos loaded his rifle and made a quick, clean kill on a good-sized deer.

We drove my brother's macho F-250 diesel King Cab across the field to get a closer look at the downed animal. We gutted the deer on site, and once it was loaded, we realized the truck had sunk to the axles in the soft, muddy field. Four-wheel drive and the big diesel engine were no match for the deep soft meadow. We were going nowhere without help. The ranch was at least twenty miles from the nearest town. Fortunately, we found a wrecking company that said they could handle the task. When the truck showed up an hour later, it was one of these rotator-style rigs that would be better classified as a crane. It was a monster, and it made pulling the truck out look easy.

The show alone was worth the thousand-dollar towing bill. Well, at least that's what I tell myself. By the time the venison was packaged and shipped back to New Hampshire, I calculated that I'd paid about fifty dollars a pound for the meat. Worth every penny. Carlos and I have very fond memories of our Montana hunting adventure.

As my kids grew older, the concept of Daddy Days evolved. Just as having flexibility in daily life is essential, it's also important when planning one-on-one time with children—and in some cases, that means expanding parameters. For instance, backpacking adventures tend to be more than one day, and while backpacking has been a fixture of Daddy Days, the trips were often two nights or more.

But the first one to really push the boundaries was Carlos. As his interest in hunting grew, I felt strongly that if he was going to kill animals, he must first learn to respect them. That meant cleaning the kill, salvaging pelts and feathers, and eating the meat. When he was still a middle school student at the Villa Augustina, the now-closed Catholic school in Goffstown, New Hampshire, Carlos planned to present at the science fair the "anatomy of a squirrel" (it turned out to be a chipmunk). This presentation included a skeleton, jars with pickled organs, a little tuxedo fur pelt, and "Casa del Sol Chipmunk Soup." As I walked into the fair after work, another parent raved to me as they were walking out: "You gotta see the kid with the chipmunk soup!" I was a particularly proud dad that night.

Our neighbor at the time, Dwayne Dorval, was a rather accomplished hunter and became quite an inspiration for Carlos. And while I had very little interest in hunting, Dwayne had so excited Carlos that soon a Daddy Day was in the works (remember, you don't necessarily do what *you* love). Hunting licenses meant hunter safety classes, so this was an example of how a "Daddy Day" can turn into *days.* Carlos and I took hunting classes together, learned about different types of firearms, hunter etiquette, and more. Carlos started hunting turkeys, and before long he wanted to target bigger game.

Carlos proposed hunting deer, but why stop there? After all, my brother, C.J., lived in Bozeman, Montana, and often regaled us with stories about hunting elk in Grasshopper Valley in the southwest part of the state. So, in 2012, we made the trip, killing two birds with one stone. I could visit my brother while Carlos could train his sights on larger game. Carlos recently reminded me how it all came to be:

> "It was only natural to suggest combining a hunting Daddy Day with a trip to visit family. I remember talking with my dad about this and trying to figure out how we would sell the idea to my mom. She was a little hesitant at first but agreed finally on the condition that I had some skin in the game. And so I began my first business selling cordwood to our neighbors. My dad taught me how to operate a chainsaw and how to swing a splitting maul. A few months later I had made enough for my plane ticket and the trip was planned.
>
> Montana is stunning. I think I told my dad almost immediately after exiting the airport that I had decided to move there. While that did not happen, my love for huge mountains and the great outdoors continued to grow. I also began to understand the value of working for something that I wanted. The trip was doubly satisfying knowing that I had paid for my ticket and "earned" this experience. And so the adventures evolved. Daddy Days were now a chance to learn new skills and experience the glory of nature with my father.

We experienced radically different weather conditions in the many locations we tried that week. One of the first days, we were in an active snowstorm in the mountains southeast of Bozeman. While we froze, we saw no elk. My brother set up his camper somewhere in Paradise Valley for us, and it was a joy just climbing the foothills above the campsite. Still, no elk. My brother joined us for a day higher in the mountains where we found tracks in the fresh powder amid the dense forest (some of those tracks were clearly grizzly bear). Fortunately, we didn't find the bear. Nor did we find the elk. At a lower elevation, Carlos did spot an elk at quite a distance, too far for the kill. Thankfully, the week did end on a high note when we visited my brother's construction project.

Uncle C.J., Carlos, and I elk hunting in Paradise Valley, Montana—near Bozeman.

If you're thinking that Montana hunting trips are only for the rich, you are right. This was a very expensive trip, and both Carlos and I had to save money to make it happen. But most of our Daddy Days are quite economical. The expenses for my most recent Daddy Day with Maria included only food for our backpacking adventure and some gas for the car. Related, the best date with my wife last summer (her suggestion) was to attend a live performance of a musical at Prescott Park in Portsmouth, New Hampshire. The tickets were a cool eight dollars, and we brought a picnic dinner.

Lesson 8: Flexibility. *When the opportunity arises, let Daddy Days grow into more than just twenty-four-hour affairs. For the most part, any parent can be generous with their time. If your kid wants to grow Daddy Days into a longer adventure, cherish it. I am so grateful that my children often challenged me this way. Overnights, campfires, multiple meals, and a variety of adventures are more likely to promote deep and meaningful conversations with loved ones.*

9 Collaboration

I was at the bottom of the ocean in sixty-foot-deep water. And I was stuck. Plenty of things *should* have been going through my mind, like: how can I free my air tank from this rock? Where are my kids? Will someone come back for me? But the one thing I could focus on was the least helpful: I'm going to die down here. Yep, this is how it ends, following an experienced leader through a tunnel on the ocean floor off the coast of Bermuda. In Davy Jones's locker.

I'm not particularly claustrophobic, I can handle my own breathing through a Scott pack, and I'm not afraid of the ocean—that is, when I'm not *stuck*. Somehow, and I still don't know how, I managed to steel my nerves and free my scuba tank, allowing me to continue the diving adventure with Carlos and Cecilia. Exploring a wrecked ship, flirting with fish, and seeing the coral here was a dream come true for all of us. And while this trip wasn't one-on-one time, it was an example of bending the rules and collaborating to make an experience possible.

My dad and my older sisters inspired this concept. After all, if our Daddy Day certificate was for twenty-four hours, then why couldn't multiple children connect them together for multiday adventures? What parent wouldn't be proud to have their children work together? Some of our most rewarding Daddy Days as children included multi-kid adventures like bushwhacking the Baxter State Park wilderness.

Cecilia, as I've mentioned, loves to swim more than anyone else in our family (she was our only child to compete in swimming). I have incredibly fond memories of playing underwater games with her, whether at the Lantern Inn with the underwater music or at Merrymeeting Lake with my favorite priest, Rev. Mark Dollard. We met Father Mark when he was assigned to St. Theresa Church in Henniker and enjoyed many years of his pastoral leadership. Every summer, he would rent a house on a New Hampshire lake (or beach) and invite us to visit. Inevitably, it would be Ceci, me, and Father Mark out swimming or playing some variation of "King of the Rock."

Given her love of water, it was no surprise Cecilia expressed an interest in scuba diving. What made it all the more auspicious was that she gravitated to it around the same time Carlos seemed interested. The timing was ideal. I was starting to feel distant from Carlos as he was advancing through high school, and scuba required that I take lessons with each of them. So, I took the class first with Carlos. Once a week for many

Carlos and Cecilia—on a joint Daddy Day—scuba diving adventure in Bermuda.

weeks, we had to take time out of our normal life and partner up in the pool. We did our first open-water dive at Dublin Lake in April with water temperature around 35 degrees.

Now, remember, one of the key ingredients to this concept is still one-on-one time. So, no sooner than Carlos and I had graduated from scuba class, I was right back there again with Cecilia doing all the same drills. Of course, it was later in the spring so our open-water dive was on Lake Winnisquam in June with more pleasant diving conditions. After it all, though, each of us had our certifications.

This was preparation for our family vacation in 2015, a cruise from Boston to Bermuda, making possible a Daddy Day two-fer with Carlos and Cecilia. We joined a small dive group for a shipwreck and cave dive in Horseshoe Bay Cove off the south side of Bermuda. Slithering through a cave that was only two feet tall, sixty feet under the water's surface, was exhilarating (well, except for that part where I thought I was about to die). It made for a thrilling adventure with both kids.

Another year Daddy Days connected to the family vacation was in 2009, our year of Freebird, as we came to call it. Linda Conti, a friend of my late sailing mentor, Pat O'Connell, had purchased a *very* used twenty-five-foot Cape Dory that she named *Freebird*. She welcomed my help as I had some aptitude for fixing old boats. It was a win-win. I helped restore Linda's boat and enjoyed it with my family in exchange (it's incredible how affordable boating can be if you are creative and willing to roll up your sleeves). It was good timing, too. Maria recalls the sea was beginning to call her name:

> In high school, I decided I wanted to take a break from hiking in order to learn to sail. My dad had grown up sailing, and had actually owned a Hobie Cat when I was young. After the Hobie flipped with me on it, I had little desire to return to that kind of

sailing, but I was interested in bigger boats. When my dad found *Freebird*, it was perfect. I got more than a weekend of learning to sail, I got a summer! I managed to become confident with the basics of sailing and navigation and by the end of that summer, my dad was confident enough in my abilities to charter sailboats in other places for our family vacations.

That summer, Maria and I made her Daddy Day a two-night sailing adventure ahead of our weeklong family vacation on the same boat. We anchored for one night near the Goslings south of Freeport and then planned to reach Orr's Island the next day and visit a candy store. In the morning when we raised our anchor, the fog was thick as pea soup. Two kayaks dutifully drifted off the stern behind us. Winds were light and this old boat had no radar and no GPS, so we were limited to our compass and a chart for navigation, but Maria and I set our course and she proudly held the tiller like Captain Jack. As we chatted and enjoyed the salty coastal Maine air, we glanced back to see that one of the kayaks was missing. Maria quickly tacked the boat back to a course 180 degrees from our prior heading. About ten minutes later, the missing kayak appeared drifting in the dense fog.

Seeing that Maria could handle the helm and navigate with a compass and chart gave me great confidence to do a weeklong cruise a month later with the whole family. The *Freebird* Daddy Day with Maria launched our sailing adventures as a family that later included bareboat charters in Puerto Rico, the Florida Keys, and Penobscot Bay, Maine.

When you really put your mind to creating an experience for a kid—or a spouse—it can lead to great ideas for your whole family, whether it's scuba diving, sailing, or any other activity. When you discover something as a duo, it's only natural sometimes that you'll want to share it more broadly. While that hasn't been true with every Daddy Day, it's something I've kept my heart open to throughout many years of adventures.

Lesson 9: Collaboration. *If your children or loved ones are inspired to join forces, that's a good thing! Chances are you will score some quality one-on-one time, too. In many cases, it's possible to carve out individual moments—like, in this instance, scuba training—that lead up to a multi-kid adventure. And in other instances, a Daddy Day can be part of, or inspire, a family vacation. Learning to work well with others is one of life's greatest gifts, and Daddy Days can help build this skill. Embrace collaboration when the opportunity presents itself, but remember the goal of Daddy Days is to grow closer to your kids.*

Dreaming

The glades of Alta and Snowbird in Utah are so steep that when you look downhill, it feels like you'll end up in the *top* of a fifty-foot fir tree if you make a mistake. They say that if you can ski the East, you can ski anywhere. New England weather is prone to result in more icy conditions, and it's true that skiers from the northeast are exceptionally talented. But some features of western skiing, like the glades of Utah, can put a tremor in the heart of the strongest East Coasters I know. Carlos is fearless on skis and is tough to keep up with. But gradually, as I learned to trust the snow conditions I was able to stick on his tail. The West is steep, but unlike in the East, you can reliably catch an edge on every turn.

Carlos is a natural at just about everything. He played a variety of sports and ran his way to the National Junior Olympics. Even when we rode horses in Puerto Rico and on a Texas dude ranch, he was the most natural and comfortable. This most certainly applied to his skiing. I coached him a little when he was young, but he quickly out-skied me. So, of course, one of his dreams (and mine!) was a Western ski trip. This surfaced during high school when I really wanted to remain connected to him. Fortunately, Renée said yes, so Carlos and I booked a trip to ski Alta, Snowbird, and Solitude in Salt Lake City. We were on a budget, so we did a Motel 8 ski-and-stay-package. And we more than got our money's worth. We even befriended a father-daughter duo who became our chauffeurs for the week, so we enjoyed free travel during our three ski days. The whole trip really was a dream come true for the two of us.

Carlos and I have long bonded over our shared love of snow sports, but recently I found a way for us to learn something new together. Over the years, I've found Renée's skiing to be slower and slower. So, a few years ago, I figured if I learned to snowboard it would be a good handicap for me to more evenly match my wife's more cautious (her word!) ski pace. I'm no expert on the board, but I can say today that I'm a solid beginner or even intermediate, and I love it. Every time I get on the board, I feel ten or twenty years younger.

With Carlos living and working in Houston, he was hungry for a skiing Daddy Day in 2023 and traveled home to make it happen. We started with a group hike up Tuckerman Ravine for what was probably the iciest day I've ever had up there. Carlos went higher into the bowl than me and skied down faster, but all had a good time and returned to the Pinkham Notch safely. This Daddy Day would not fit within a twenty-four-hour container (especially since Carlos came all the way from Houston), so we then drove the scenic but bumpy Route 16 over to Rangeley, Maine,

Carlos quickly shows the old buck how to snowboard at Saddleback.

where I would challenge Carlos to learn something new. Carlos had never been on a snowboard, so I put him on some loaner equipment and proceeded to "teach" him how it was done. We were fortunate to have six inches of fresh snowfall the first day, and the second was beautiful and sunny. By the end of day one, Carlos had already caught up to my skill level. By day two, he surpassed me.

This is one of the moguls we hit in the life of being a dad: your kiddos will best you in many ways. If your heart is in the right place, it should only give you joy. Carlos easily ran faster than me by the time he was twelve. He's better at running, riding horses, skateboarding, shooting, kiteboarding, skiing, and with two days learning compared to my two seasons, he's better at snowboarding, too. I couldn't be more proud of him.

While each Daddy Days is unique, most have a theme of adventure mixed in and many of those adventures have helped me and my family learn new things. But in other instances, the goal is less about adventure and more about making someone's dream come true. No doubt, Carlos and I checked a box in Utah, but it was in some ways an easy ask because we both love skiing. In other instances I've had to set aside my own passions to accommodate someone else's dreams.

Early in our marriage, Renée dreamt of a romantic getaway to Quebec City. I have a relatively modest engineering income, so we were certainly not going to be staying at the Fairmont Le Château Frontenac. The deal I struck with my bride was to car-camp on Île d'Orléans, an island in the Saint Lawrence River, for one night, followed by a bed and breakfast stay in the city for night number two. While I admit that sleeping in the car is not very romantic, it made the next night all the sweeter. And while we were in the city, we saw a phenomenal outdoor performance of Cirque du Soleil that featured acrobats suspended from highway overpasses. It was jaw-dropping. Renée and I returned home so enthusiastic about our trip to Quebec that it inspired our family vacation the following summer.

Morning sun and rested campers near our car-campsite on Île d'Orléans in Quebec.

While this one wasn't a Daddy Day, it counted as what we came to call "Tarzan Days"—a concept we'll explore in more detail later. Essentially, these follow the same format of Daddy Days but rather they are husband-and-wife adventures—sort of like mini-honeymoons. They also provide an opportunity for me to focus on my wife's desires.

For many years, Renée also dreamt of visiting Colonial Williamsburg. She is a huge history buff and likes to soak in museums. We even scheduled it so that we could join in for a tremendous ball with formal attire. This was scheduled for Memorial Day weekend following 9/11, so the TSA was experiencing growing pains. We stood in line for security for over sixty minutes and got to our gate just as the door had closed. The next flight with availability for us was not until the evening, so our chances of attending the ball were shot. Instead, we spent the day in Cambridge touring Longfellow House (where Washington based his Revolutionary War leadership) and lunching nearby as we waited for our evening plane.

When we finally made it to Williamsburg, I overdosed quickly on the museums and speakers, but this trip wasn't just about my preferences. I knew it meant a lot to Renée, so I tried my best to be a good sport. And I even enjoyed some of it! The fifes and drum corps that performed on Memorial Day might be the best live music I've ever experienced. Still, as part of our hindsight analysis, Renée and I agreed that perhaps on the next trip to Williamsburg, we'll insert a round of golf as a break from the museums. Ultimately, I'm human, and while I've done my best to make dreams come true as part of both Daddy and Tarzan days, it can prove to be a challenge.

Lesson 10: Dreaming. *Sometimes you need to let go of your own dreams to focus on those of the people you love. My pastor, Rev. Dennis Audet, once challenged our congregation that when we receive the Eucharist (us Catholics believe that Jesus Christ is truly present in communion), we should not only meditate that we have just received the real body and blood of Christ but that we should also become Christ, for others. Yeah, the guy that literally laid down his life for all of us imperfect mortals. Jesus would do anything for us. We should do the same for our children and loved ones. Be open to new ideas and activities—even the ones you don't love. It's one of the best ways to show your family that you are for real. Daddy Days, done right, should be a time for making dreams come true together.*

11 Humility

My favorite character in the 1961 film *King of Kings* is the Roman centurion Lucius. He is handsome and charming. He is presented as a faithful military man with a body of iron, nerves of steel, and a heart of gold. When Pontius Pilate quizzes Lucius about the greatest character fault in men, Lucius quickly responds: "Vanity!" It's taken decades for this concept to really sink into my thick skull. One of the turning points was when a close friend kindly told me that I was intimidating. I had never thought of myself this way, perhaps because I lacked some of the self-awareness that comes with humility. Life has been good to me and I've worked hard on all fronts. I've enjoyed success in sports, school, work, and marriage—all of which, when taken together, does tend to bolster the ego and lead to vanity. I know today I could spend more time practicing humility, and thankfully, some Daddy Days have forced me to do so.

In 2016, I thought I was helping Carlos find his future home. He'd just graduated from high school, and I was feeling distant from him. He was solidly into pot and the related culture. At the time, Colorado was leading the charge with the legalization of marijuana, and I knew that Carlos would also enjoy the general vibe of the area. So, we booked a four-day visit to the Centennial State. Typical of my favorite vacations and adventures, there wasn't a firm plan.

We began with a night at an Airbnb in Denver. The next day, we found an incredible skateboard park downtown. Now, I'm not a skateboarder, and at fifty, I cannot say that I was tempted to start doing concrete wipeouts. And I'm typically not a very good spectator, but I will confess that I really did enjoy watching Carlos and others in the skateboard parks. In four quick days, we also hit parks in Boulder, Leadville, Aspen, Telluride, and Breckenridge. We just happened to hit Breckenridge on the day of an international skateboard competition, so the skills exhibited were incredible. I had never seen fifteen-foot-deep swimming-pool-style skate parks. It was astonishing.

Trying to pull this off on a budget, Carlos and I car camped one of the nights in Grand Junction. We were both very impressed with the Colorado outdoors-focused vibe. In Telluride, we quickly met a local who at one point knew my brother, C.J., an outstanding skier nicknamed Turbo. We toured Red Rocks, explored mountains, and Carlos completely scored when he found us a log-cabin B&B with an amazing host family. I was falling in love with the state and thought for sure Carlos would be inspired to move there. I was wrong. But at least my son knew that I loved him enough to bring him to a place that I thought he would enjoy. I had no regrets.

While I did enjoy the trip, the four days were trying. I thought this trip would inspire Carlos to dream big. Instead, I watched my son hang out with what I perceived to be low-motivated skateboarders (though, I admit, they had real talent). While the tricks were impressive, I didn't find it very inspiring. When we visited Aspen, Carlos openly declared that he was thoroughly disgusted by the opulence. (I admit it's over the top, but it doesn't disgust me—it's just not my world.) While I attended church, he stayed at the skateboard park. I recall crying as I was so disappointed that he could not give me an hour when I was giving him four days. It was hard to accept. My son and I may have lots in common, but at eighteen, he clearly was not smoking the "I Love Jesus" side of John Turner.

On the trip that I had hoped would bring us together, I was feeling even more distant. This hit a climax at the Denver airport security for our return trip. Carlos opted to wear his grungiest outfit so the security team naturally targeted him for a screening. As they frisked his baggy clothes,

I worried we might not be returning home together. Carlos managed to get through, but not without a lot of anger. It put a significant damper on our trip and was a reminder to me that while we have a great deal in common, he has his own ideas for life, and I had some growing to do in the areas of acceptance and love of his choices.

Summit of Mount Evans—in the middle of our Colorado Daddy Days.

Carlos knows that I love him deeply. I am so incredibly grateful that he recently told me that he has always felt my love for him, because I have genuinely tried to support whatever he was interested in. When I asked Carlos to reflect on that Colorado trip for this book, he was initially reluctant. Later, he shared the following:

> Colorado was an interesting time for me. While I loved my parents deeply, I also heavily disagreed with some things they believed in. This trip was a bridge across that divide, and showed

me that even with our stark belief differences, my dad and I can enjoy each other's company and make unforgettable memories. It was a formative time for me as I was trying to figure out my own beliefs and how to live them in a way that was still harmonious with my parents. That process is ongoing but my love for my parents is stronger than ever. Showing that you do not always need to agree in order to love and care about those around you.

Even in the hardest moments, Daddy Days have remained an opportunity for us to disconnect and take deep conversational dives together—even on subjects about which we don't agree. While Colorado tested us, it didn't damage the bond we share. In fact, two of the Daddy Days that followed the trip to Colorado are among the best trips Carlos and I have shared.

Both were backpacking trips. The first was to the beautiful Jay Peak in northern Vermont. I recall a relaxed drive on all back roads—up the

Backpacking and camping on Jay Peak.

Connecticut River valley—deliberately avoiding the interstates. We hiked to the summit and camped out just below it. We enjoyed a campfire and deep conversation. The food with Carlos is always healthy and delicious. It was one of our most simple Daddy Days, yet felt rewarding to take a mini-retreat together.

On another trip very similar to Jay Peak, we wanted to disappear into the wilderness and build a shelter together. Carlos was framing houses at the time and was feeling the intensity of his super physical work. And I think I may have tweaked my shoulder or back just before this one, so we agreed that we could both be very content with sleeping in a tent.

We were proud of ourselves for summiting Bond Cliff in the White Mountains until a young woman came along and shared that she was completing the Pemi Loop that day (31.2 miles, nine peaks, 9,724 feet of elevation gain) and that she is working on her "grid" (all New Hampshire Four-thousand Footers, every month, repeat for a year!). Carlos and I suddenly felt quite wimpy (talk about humility). But we quickly got over

Bond Cliff and camping on the Pemigewasset together.

it as our tent site was at the edge of the East Branch of the Pemigewasset and we enjoyed a glorious stargazing night above our campfire. All ingredients for an amazing Daddy Day in my book: outdoor adventure, a good workout, healthy food, technology free, and, most importantly, the company of my son.

Lesson 11: Humility. *Listen to Tim McGraw's song "Humble and Kind." Consider the challenge each of us faces every day to jettison arrogance and vanity and practice humility. And then bring humility to your relationships with your children. What might they be struggling with today? How might you learn from them? How can you better support their dreams and decisions, even if those decisions aren't ones you would make yourself?*

PART 3

DOING HARD THINGS

12 Determination

Around the time Cecilia was approaching driving age, I had somehow convinced Renée to let *me* buy a used BMW 535. *Noche*, as we called her, was the most incredible car I have ever owned. Beautiful, quiet, powerful, comfortable, and agile. So, why should I be surprised that my sixteen-year-old daughter told me that she wanted a Mercedes Benz C300 as her first car? After all, Daddy had had a cool ride. Renée and I tried to reason with her that she should really buy a Honda Accord or Toyota Camry, but arguing with a teenage girl can be futile. Plus, she was a highly-motivated, mature teen, and she wanted to take the lead on this process.

We brokered a deal that Renée and I would match Ceci's savings dollar for dollar toward the new car, but our contribution would end at four thousand dollars. Ceci worked three jobs and quickly scored the matching four thousand and then some. Most ten-year-old, one-hundred-thousand-mile C300s were going for twelve thousand dollars or more at the time. We test drove many together, always with Cecilia doing the negotiating. She eventually found a black beauty at a Lexus dealership in Bedford, New Hampshire. I worked hard to keep my male ego in check and let my sixteen-year-old do all the talking with the salesman, who seemed rather shocked when, during the test drive, he learned her age. He said that he would have guessed she was twenty. Well, twenty minutes later, my daughter had convinced him to sell her the car with a fourteen-thousand-dollar sticker price for ten thousand dollars. It was way less than I would have asked for, and I was proud of her for being so bold. She was determined to get that car, and thanks to her stick-to-itiveness she did just that.

It's no surprise that the same determined lady knocked out her criminal justice degree at Saint Anselm College in three years. She did this by working hard, taking summer classes, and avoiding the party scene. When she asked about doing a spring break cruise with me for her senior year Daddy Day, it seemed like a reasonable request—and one she'd earned.

We booked our cruise and flights during the era when post-Covid travel was really starting to ramp up again. Sadly, the airline canceled our flight with less than twelve hours of notice. We booked seats on another airline, which also subsequently canceled. Our cruise would be leaving the port in Cape Canaveral, Florida, in twenty-four hours. I knew this trip meant a lot to Cecilia, so we decided to book a one-way car rental and drive from New Hampshire to Florida. In hindsight, it was not realistic, as the drive to Florida would easily take more time than we had available. Technically, just looking at a GPS, you *could* argue that we might have made it in time—but when you account for traffic, bathroom breaks, and exhaustion, we were toast.

Still, this may have been my all-time best Daddy Day with Cecilia—and certainly the longest. The drive from New Hampshire to Florida forced us to engage in conversation. Somewhat like the concept that camping together brings people closer because there are challenges, long car rides have a similar effect—especially one with a critical deadline. As we approached New York City on I-95, traffic crawled and vendors hawked water bottles, roses, fruit, and God knows what else. We had only driven a few hours but were already realizing we were doomed.

As we drove, we contacted our travel agent to see if we could join the cruise on day two at Nassau. Somehow, despite all the pitches from the cruise line about being the masters of fun, they didn't think it would be particularly *fun* if we joined them a day late. Ceci and I gradually realized that our dream was going down the tubes and that we would need to resign ourselves to some land-based fun instead. I recall that we accepted this outcome in Georgia, and decided we should get some sleep rather than doze off and crash a rental car into the forest.

As we entered Florida, our hopes of a tropical spring break vacation were dampened by mediocre weather, too. When we finally got to the beach in Saint Augustine, there were showers. We continued south to Flagler Beach, where the sun broke through and we were able to catch some rays on the beach (and of course we jumped in). Our adventure continued in Daytona and then on to Orlando, where we attempted to visit Disney. Alas, we ended up at Disney Springs, where all the non-planners end up. We had a good time, but this one left both of us with a bit of sadness that we failed to get on the cruise ship. Still, it was a lesson in determination and patience. Cecilia and I did enjoy our time. We hit a bunch of memorable Orlando sites, like a wax museum, aquarium, and other amusement parks. Most importantly, we enjoyed lots of quality time.

A cruise Daddy Day turned into Orlando Adventures.

A year later, Cecilia and I agreed that we should try again. By 2024, she was living and working in Houston, so she was now a quick drive from the cruise ships. This time, Renée would join us. Cecilia and I took a snorkeling excursion together, and aboard the ship we enjoyed the water-park with the tweens, the hot tubs, and bar drinks with the Boomers. Renée is not a party animal, so she and Cecilia enjoyed trivia games and we all enjoyed "family dinners" together each evening. As we sat on that boat, though, it was impossible not to remember how determined we'd been the year before, and how ultimately it led to this new family memory. "If that is not love and dedication I don't know what is," Cecilia said recently when I asked her about our efforts to make a cruise happen.

Cecilia finally gets her cruise Daddy Day—and yes—we still played in the water-park with the tweens.

Determination is a skill that develops over time, and it's one that is essential for making Daddy Days happen. Whether your kid is three or thirty, there will always be obstacles in the way of scheduling these days. When our flight to Florida was canceled, we could have easily just canceled the whole trip. But what message would that have given my daughter? If I can't have an easy trip, it's not worth it? If you're stuck in a bad relationship, you should suck it up and take it? If you've tried online dating for six months and it's not going well, you should give it up? I have no regrets that Cecilia and I agreed together to persevere and make the most of our time together—and I have no doubt it was a result of our determination.

Lesson 12: Determination. *In a world that worships immediate gratification, teaching our children the combined skills of determination and patience is paramount. Many of the best things in life take time, and often they don't happen on the first try. Whether it's school, job applications, or literally building a relationship with your kids, don't throw in the towel if you're struggling initially. Be patient. Remain determined.*

Generosity

Tithing has always been something I've taken seriously. Less than a year into my marriage to Renée, I severed my professional umbilical cord—in other words, I left my job at Texas Instruments as a technical sales engineer. When I first hit Renée with the idea, she was rather disappointed. "What? I married this young engineer with a company car, his own (very humble) house, a steady job and free Red Sox tickets, and he is going to throw it away to start his own business?" Yes, I was excited to create adventure in my professional life—not just my personal life. I had met Alan Mooney of Criterium Engineers when I was in the eighth grade, and many years later I remembered how much his building and engineering knowledge impressed me. I quickly signed up to become the owner of the New Hampshire Franchise of Criterium Engineers, a company specializing in building inspection engineering.

Fortunately, Renée did ultimately support the decision, and we always gave generously to our church and many other causes. Early in my Criterium-Turner Engineers business, it was stressful to look ahead on my calendar and see no jobs scheduled. It probably took me at least fifteen years to get used to the idea that the work would keep coming. I have become convinced that the more generous I am, the more work flows in. I will never be rich, I know this. We are still working to pay off our mortgage, but for thirty years of self-employment, we've never been hungry—a realization that helps me believe in the promise of America.

In the early 2000s, business was doing fine. We had purchased a nice new Chevy Suburban for Renée that we called the *Polar Bear*—a perfect rig for family adventures. The following year, I bought the nicest pickup truck I had ever owned, a Dodge 1500 Quad Cab with the Hemi engine. She was pretty and macho, and she sounded awesome.

That truck was about six months old when I took Maria for a Daddy Day. We started our day at Six Flags in Springfield, Massachusetts, for some fun on the big roller coasters. We concluded that day in standard Turner fashion—packing many things into one outing—with a second adventure, a hike up Massachusetts's tallest mountain, Greylock. The idea was to camp near the summit, so we parked the truck at the trailhead around 5 P.M.

Just as we were about to start backpacking, a grungy young couple showed up in the parking lot. I knew Mount Greylock was on the Appalachian Trail, and I immediately recognized these two as thru-hikers. For anyone that has hiked sections of the Appalachian Trail, thru-hikers (people hiking the entire 2,190-mile trail) are easy to spot—typically you smell them first. Many have long hair. The guys have beards. They have socks and underwear dangling from their backpack as they try to dry the laundry they washed in a pond. I didn't *need* these two to explain their endeavor, but they told us they really needed food and asked about the nearest store. As I thought back to our drive in, I realized it was probably ten miles away—not what any thru-hiker wants to hear at the end of a long day. Now, I have a big heart, but I really didn't want to delay my hiking start with Maria. I felt called to help them somehow.

So, I tossed them the keys to my brand new truck and asked them to return them at an agreed-upon campsite near the top of the mountain (they had already set up camp there before hiking down for provisions). It was a little risky, but a good example that if everyone on Planet Earth rolled this way, all of our lives might be better. The couple did exactly as I asked. They returned the keys to me after dark on the mountain. Maria and I enjoyed summiting the next morning and returned to find my truck in perfect condition. Even better, they left us a bag of Reese's Pieces with a note that read: *We have experienced lots of trail magic on the AT, but YOU are the trail God!* It was really no big deal, but it was what they needed at the time.

The act was spontaneous on my part. I didn't do it to demonstrate to my ten-year-old daughter that I was capable of generosity and trusting strangers. I did it because I believe fundamentally that letting go and being generous is essential to creating heaven on Earth. Sure, some will point out that I could have lost my truck or been liable for an accident, but experience has taught me that more often than not people *really* are good—and it's a lesson that I try to pass on to my kids, too.

A few years later, I was attending a homebuilder networking event. I met a gentleman named Steve Labbe, who ultimately inspired me to visit his BNI (Business Network International) chapter called Granite State Money Makers. This group is dedicated to a concept they call "Givers Gain." In other words: If I give you business, then you'll want to give me business. I count Steve among my greatest friends, and we've been sharing the BNI Kool-Aid now for fifteen years together. When Steve served as president of the chapter, he inspired a name change to "BNI Wolf Pack." We track real results, and over the years our fellow members have credited both Steve and me with around five million dollars in "Thank You for Closed Business!" This means that I referred a client to another member, they sold a job, and then remembered to enter these sales dollars into our tracking system.

We meet every week and work hard to get to know fellow members and find good referrals for them. One week, I might refer a roofing project to someone I know. Another week, I might bring an unemployed friend into the group to help them find a job. We constantly work to help others, to coach young business owners, to give great referrals. It cultivates a generous heart—one that reminds us to give to others when our fortunes allow it.

Lesson 13: Generosity. *Reflect on this message from the prayer of Saint Francis: "For it is in giving that we receive." Daddy Days give us opportunities to demonstrate generosity in action. Give your children the chance to see you drive politely and responsibly, tip generously, interact kindly with others, and share resources. You don't have to give away your new truck, but you do need to share joy and love with every person you encounter.*

Grit

When I was too little to tag along, I recall my brother, C.J., would set off to Maine to canoe the Allagash Wilderness Waterway on multiday trips. Occasionally, my sister Mary would join him and, being too young, I would be left behind. The Allagash River is a bucket list adventure for adrenaline junkies in the Northeast. It's one of the few rivers in the U.S. that drains north toward the Canadian border, offering access to wide swaths of remote forest. Paddling through the wilderness area requires one to cross lakes, run class II rapids (or portage around them), and in the summer months, endure armies of ravenous mosquitoes. For most people, the adventure requires four or five nights of camping with no provisions along the way. I see why it made sense to leave me at home. Still, it fueled my fire.

When we were both game for a serious adventure and we agreed it was time for us to tackle the river together. Early June seemed a reasonable time, so we cruised to Maine and paid a guide to transport us and our *Cool Runnings* canoe (yes, named after the movie) upriver to John's Bridge between Round Pond and Churchill Lake. Aside from a stiff headwind, the journey began pleasantly—sunny and 60 degrees.

Our first night was also a relatively easy experience. Carlos demonstrated his survival prowess by catching wild brook trout, which we cooked over the campfire. He slept in his lightweight hammock while I enjoyed the abundant space in our four-man tent. I can't say that I expected frost that night. It was pretty much a full-time job to keep the campfire going to stay warm, which was all good. It gave us plenty of time to talk. College. Girls. Framing houses. Dreams. Hopes. Fears. To be clear, there was also plenty of time for pure silence as well. I am somewhat brave, but that wilderness is vast—and I'm not sure I would have felt comfortable being there alone. With Carlos, I was at ease. Even when we were silent, I cherished his company.

Conditions were cooler on day two, but we still made it to our target destination for the day: Round Pond. We enjoyed the entire lake to ourselves and, of course, jumped in. We then explored the scariest fire tower I've ever climbed, about one hundred feet high with a very light frame. Carlos is nothing if not brave, but even *he* agreed the climb was sketchy. We could see south to Mount Katahdin and Baxter State Park, north to Canada, and a panorama of abundant wilderness. We could also see a patchwork of forest where trees had been harvested and planted and were in various stages of regrowth—a reminder of the logging industry still so prominent in Maine.

On day three, our weather turned ugly, cold, and wet. Making campfires and keeping them going became a chore—but also an essential one to stay warm. We retired early as the rain made paddling conditions miserable. Showers grew to downpours and temperatures must have been no more than 40 degrees. About halfway through that night, Carlos unzipped the tent and told me that his sleeping bag was soaked and he was freezing. It was time to join me inside my dry sleeping bag. Talk about father-son bonding. In the morning, Carlos ventured down to the river and came running back to tell me our canoe was gone. After watching my jaw drop, he disclosed the prank, which had its intended effect. Losing a canoe fifteen miles out on the Allagash would have been a disaster. Fortunately, the rain let up and we continued our paddle downriver. We eventually made it out of the woods, but we were mentally exhausted by the time we emerged.

This was not the hardest Daddy Day physically, but it absolutely built grit. Single overnight trips are relatively easy: if your gear gets wet, you know that you have a hot shower, dry clothes, and a warm bed back home. Multiday excursions become more mentally challenging, reflective of a Japanese Shinto practice called *misogi*. Historically, a misogi was a ritual of purification that involved making a pilgrimage to a freezing waterfall and immersing oneself under it. In modern times, the concept has been broadened to mean doing something that is extremely difficult every year—something so hard you're not sure you'll accomplish it. The goal is to test the limits.

I first encountered the concept while reading *Comfort Crisis* by author and journalist Michael Easter. In the book, Easter makes the case that personal growth is inherently tied to doing hard things. He attributes the modern understanding of misogi to one of the world's top sports scientists, Dr. Marcus Elliot. There are two rules for a modern misogi, he says: 1. Make it really hard. 2. Don't die. In vivid detail Easter describes a misogi-like trip he takes deep into the Arctic, where he encounters frigid temperatures, no cell service, and crushing solitude. And while my own adventures have not been so extreme, many of the Daddy Days I've shared with my kids have been in the spirit of the misogi.

As I read Easter's book, I was reminded of Christ, who spent forty days in the desert as he prepared himself for his passion and crucifixion. And while none of us today are perhaps preparing ourselves for something so magnificent, the wilderness—and its accompanying challenges—can be a great teacher. Joseph Ratzinger, better known as Pope Benedict XVI, who led the Catholic Church from 2005 until 2013, offered an incisive adage about growing beyond our comfort zones. "The world offers you comfort," he once said. "But you were not made for comfort. You were made for greatness."

Lesson 14: Grit. *Escaping your comfort zone is essential in order to grow as an individual, as a spouse, and as a parent. Remember what Pope Benedict said: "You were made for greatness." As you focus on a relationship with your children, think about how you can push each other to leave comfort behind and embrace something truly difficult. You don't have to plan a misogi-like challenge, but don't settle for what's easy.*

Bravery

Perhaps the most impressive endurance athletes who have ever lived are found not in East Africa, but in the Copper Canyons of the Sierra Madre Occidental mountain range in the Mexican state of Chihuahua. Native Mexican runners from the Tarahumara tribe—depicted in Christopher McDougall's 2009 book *Born to Run*—often wear nothing on their feet but primitive sandals called huaraches (they feature leather straps and rubber soles made from old tires), and they run at blistering speeds. As McDougall's book depicts, the Tarahumara can cover hundreds of miles at the pace of Olympic athletes—all the while demonstrating an uncanny ability to avoid injury.

McDougall reveals the secrets that keep these Mexican runners so healthy (and speedy), and he helps runners like me understand important lessons about endurance and longevity. Along the way, he makes a compelling case that running is a pursuit that—if done properly—can be enjoyed for a lifetime. In a quote he attributes to Jack Kirk, a renowned runner known as the "Dipsea Demon," McDougall shares a witticism I remember every time I lace up my sneakers: "You don't stop running because you get old. You get old because you stop running."

I've been an inconsistent runner throughout my life. I ran cross country as a high schooler to train for cross-country ski racing. I then ran at lunchtime for a few years when working for Texas Instruments. Then I dropped it for decades as I "ran" my own business. And now, pushing sixty, I am inspired by my runner-born-again-son to get back into it.

However, one cardiovascular pursuit that has remained a constant in my life is hiking—particularly on the rugged trails of northern New England. The physical challenge presented by mountain climbing is part of my DNA. So, too, is my tendency to challenge people around me. I've always found great joy helping others push through physical exertion and experience the joy that comes with achieving a goal.

I recently looked through all of the adventure photos I've accumulated over the years, and I realized I've visited one location perhaps more than any other: Tuckerman Ravine, the legendary glacial cirque on the southeast side of Mount Washington. Climbing into Tuckerman Ravine in any season is strenuous, but I often choose to do it in late winter or early spring, almost always with a plan to hike the bowl and ski down. Each year for the past twenty years, I've hiked it—and I've introduced dozens of people to the intensity and majesty of Mount Washington's most iconic feature.

There are only a handful of people who have hiked and skied Tuckerman Ravine with me more than five times. Two of them are Carlos and Maria. To reach the top of the ravine when it is covered in snow and ice is exhausting, exhilarating, and frankly terrifying. Very few people feel a need to experience it more than once. Still, I'm not surprised that Maria and Carlos have been up to the challenge nearly every time I got the itch. Over the course of decades, they have become rugged and indefatigable adventure partners upon whom I can trust in the wilderness, and while none of us can run like the Tarahumara we are committed to long journeys underfoot.

As you read anecdotes of the various wilderness challenges I've undertaken with my children, you might think I am masochistic. You might think I push my kids beyond their limits, or that I sound like David Goggins, the former Navy Seal and Army Ranger who became an adventure athlete and gained fame as a motivational speaker. And to that, I might plead guilty. I could not be more proud of the physical and mental toughness of Carlos and Maria in particular, who perform everyday tasks with discipline and rigor. However, just because I'm eager for an adventure does not mean I'm not occasionally frightened during our pursuits.

My dad can no longer answer questions like this, but I suspect he was pretty scared when he had a stranger drop two of his kids onto a pond in the middle of Baxter State Park in Maine. I also suspect that he was as scared as I was when we moved that septic tank to Isle au Haut in his small lake fishing boat. Fear and bravery are not mutually exclusive—and I know my dad was brave. He taught me to be brave, as well.

Was I scared when Carlos was ripping down the crazy steep glades at Snowbird? Yes. Was I scared when Maria and I sailed *Freebird* out of the harbor in Maine for the first time? Definitely. Was I scared when Carlos and I were ripping down corduroy ice (a northeast ski area phenomenon generated by snow groomers followed by below freezing temperatures) at Saddleback on snowboards? Of course. I'm not suggesting being suicidal (remember the second rule of the misogi: Don't die). But I am suggesting that you undertake things that seem scary and push you beyond your perceived limits.

Still, it's important to remember that every relationship is different. Cecilia, who has been on plenty of hikes with me, does not seek out physical challenges in the way her siblings do. While she is quite tolerant of my constant need to stay in motion, she's less likely to strap skis to her back and walk uphill. And so I challenge myself to find other ways to create closeness in our relationship. I often remind myself that I must love my kids for who they are, and when it comes time to plan a day together, I prioritize activities in which they can find joy. I am still continually impressed by the ways Cecilia pursues excellence—even if it isn't in endurance sports.

There are times when I could be more mindful about testing the limits of those around me, but I do believe that in many cases physical challenges are good for the mind, and they can translate to everyday tasks. As Goggins says: "Don't stop when you're tired. Stop when you're done."

Lesson 15: Bravery. *If you want to raise children that can handle the tough things in life, take them backpacking up mountains. Get soaking wet and cold in the pouring rain. Get eaten alive by mosquitoes. Take a dip in that freezing cold mountain pond. Shut off your phone. Build a campfire. Build a shelter. Bring plenty of food. Bring a water filter. Bring dry clothes. I guarantee you will create memories that will last a lifetime and both you and your kids will learn lessons. And it will serve them well whether they are a soldier, a teacher, a carpenter, a counselor, a firefighter, or a cosmetologist.*

Taking Care of the Crew

Skies were overcast with a gentle five-knot breeze when I directed my crew—my immediate family—to hoist the anchor and raise the sails. Both the main and jib sails were high in the air as our thirty-foot sloop, sailing just off the west side of Culebra, an island east of Puerto Rico, cruised inland toward the village where I hoped to attend church. That's when all hell broke loose.

I'd drained both batteries in our chartered sailboat the previous day, which meant I couldn't start the engine. And having no battery, our radio was dead—which prevented me from checking the weather. Within minutes of raising the sails, the skies darkened. The wind picked up, quickly reaching what felt like tropical storm conditions. Frothy waves crashed over the bow. Conditions grew chaotic so quickly that there was no chance we could reef the sails and get the boat under better control. My experienced hand was on the tiller, but even with my years of sailing there was no way to avoid several near knock-down events (meaning the boat tips and the sails hit the water).

Owing to its heavy, fixed keel, our boat was sturdy enough not to capsize, and fortunately the squall only lasted five or ten minutes, though it felt like an eternity. The winds lightened as heavy rain crashed down upon the deck, so we were able to bring the sloop under control again, sail into the harbor, and set anchor. When we arrived, I looked at the faces of my family members and I knew I'd put my crew—the people I love most—in a dangerous situation.

Taking care of the crew is an important part of any adventure, be it on water or land. My late friend and sailing mentor J.J. "Pat" O'Connell, a Marine who served in Vietnam, reinforced this lesson when he was teaching me how to handle sailboats in my youth. Pat held strong opinions about nearly everything, and he was always more than happy to let you know about it. Why Notre Dame lost the last football game. Why Volvos are the best car on the planet. Why National hardware is superior to Stanley. Why you should vote for Bill Clinton. And, most interesting to me at the time, why Ericson sailboats were the best.

While I was in high school, Pat would often take me out on his twenty-eight-foot Ericson and show me the ropes—literally and figuratively. He taught myriad lessons, most of which were inspired by his time in the United States Marine Corps. How to tie two bow-lines. How to shut down a diesel engine. How to pick up a mooring. But one lesson he repeated more than any other is that it's a captain's responsibility to keep his crew safe.

I wasn't proud of what happened to my family in Puerto Rico, and I'm grateful it wasn't worse. But I am proud to say, while taking care of the crew has been a lifelong challenge, this type of event is not my norm. Most of the people I've adventured with will admit that my preferred recreational pursuits are typically challenging, and occasionally soggy, but not life threatening. I firmly believe that outdoor adventures should be rugged, and I'm convinced that adversity leads to growth. I want my adventure buddies to experience exhilaration—but I don't want them to die from hypothermia (or anything else, for that matter).

One of my *better* moments taking care of the crew was on Tuckerman Ravine a few winters ago. I had set my heart on a midwinter date hoping for some powder conditions. The forecast for the planned day was calling for record cold temperatures—perhaps lows of -40 degrees Fahrenheit on top of Mount Washington and highs, even at Pinkham Notch Lodge, of just 10 degrees. So, a few people stressed this was a terribly bad idea—and those words of caution were not lost on me. Mount Washington is notorious for hiker and skier deaths due to rapid weather changes and avalanches, and I respect that mountain greatly.

But I had actually checked the weather this time (I do learn, albeit slowly) and what I saw in the forecast was sunshine and light winds. After all, I'm terminally optimistic. My small crew of young adults arrived at the parking lot about 9 A.M. and we all shuddered when we got out of our cars. But we quickly assembled gear and started hiking. By the time we hit HoJos (the ranger station at the bottom of the Tuckerman Ravine bowl where you decide if conditions are safe enough to venture into the avalanche zone), it felt like Colorado—clear blue skies and brilliant sunshine—so that all could comfortably hang out on the deck and enjoy our victory drinks with bare hands.

I not only enjoyed the victory drink that day, I also enjoyed the victory in being bold about *not* canceling our adventure just because it was going to be cold. I've often said that I prefer 10 degrees and sunny to 40 degrees and rain. My crew at Tuckerman that year agreed that it was a great call. And it was one of many trips to Tuckerman Ravine that concluded with a simple ski down the John Sherburne ski trail (no bowl skiing that day), a moderately difficult, but not life-threatening, trail through the woods.

If you want to be successful with Daddy Days, you need to at least think about what you are getting into. When Carlos and I paddled the Allagash River in Maine, it was early June. I was surprised the first night when temperatures plunged and we awoke to frost. Fortunately, Carlos is tough and was barely fazed, but we both were pretty chilled the next few days. I recall spending most of one rainy, raw day just working hard to keep the campfire going to keep our hands warm. I think Carlos would agree that this was not a failure of taking care of the crew, but rather a challenge we enjoyed together during a hardcore Daddy Day.

When discussing this topic with Maria recently, she recalled how I consistently would bring macaroni and cheese on her backpacking trips. If it was getting cool, she would snuggle into the sleeping bag while I cooked. In the morning, I would boil water and deliver nice hot chocolate into the tent—so she could stay in her sleeping bag cocoon. Renée has also reminded me many times that the only reason she could tolerate family camping adventures is that I would own the cooking and clean up. Taking care of the crew can be a simple thing like providing drinks and a snack for the car ride.

At the end of the day, Pat, my mentor and the tough-loving Marine, was right: Taking care of the crew must always be a priority, and it really boils down to behaving like a gentleman. Listen carefully to the needs of your crew and be kind to those you love.

Lesson 16: Take care of the crew—always. *Daddy Days should be memorable. They should not be life threatening. There's a delicate balance between high thrill and pushing people over the edge. Plan ahead, bring proper supplies and plentiful food, and do everything you can to ensure that adventures are enjoyable—not dangerous.*

17 Nutrition

It seems that every ethnicity claims food as the center of their identity. Italian, French, Greek, Cuban, Japanese, Mexican, Jamaican—even Texans! For so many people food is an essential part of their cultural fabric. To me, food is less about cultural background and more about a simple natural law: God designed us to need a continuous source of fuel, and the moment you start to adventure seriously, the calorie demand goes up. Over the years, I've developed a not-so-pithy doctrine I refer to as the "Four Most Important Rules of Awesome Food according to JT." It's a simple formula that goes like this:

1. The food is prepared by someone else.
2. It is eaten outdoors.
3. It is enjoyed atop a mountain.
4. It is enjoyed with family and friends.

Culinary pursuits must be managed uniquely with each Daddy Day giftee. With both Carlos and Maria, we are more likely to be headed off into the wilderness, and thus the food shopping to prepare for the adventure is more crucial. Of course, everyone knows that you should not shop on an empty stomach, so we often hit a breakfast café before the grocery store.

A dozen eggs and a pound of bacon for a generous Daddy Day camping breakfast with nine-year-old Carlos.

Now, food shopping isn't my specialty. Our family generally settled into traditional roles. Often, Renée did the grocery shopping and cooking while I renovated our homes. So, what landed in the grocery cart shopping with me was quite different from routine trips to the store with Renée. In the early years of adventure meal planning, Carlos and I might purchase a dozen eggs and a pound of bacon for one breakfast for the two of us. I recall Renée giving me grief as Carlos was growing into husky clothing at age eleven. But his active nature and genes quickly shaped his body with six-pack abs atop the legs of a gazelle.

Two winters ago, as Carlos and I were returning from our snowboarding adventure at Saddleback, I was ready for a couple of 99-cent heart-attack burgers. Carlos challenged me instead to hit the grocery store, where he guided our selection of cheese, nuts, olives, kombucha tea, and other healthy foods. He suggested that by reducing carbs and sugars, I would experience more long-term energy and would be less likely to have a sugar crash. He was right on, and inspired me that day to make more healthy food choices going forward.

Maria and I have a special little tradition of our own as part of these pre-adventure grocery store visits. We always select something different. For many years, we've tried fruits that are new to us—or at least fruits that we do not regularly consume. But, as Maria explains, these adventures also helped her sharpen her aptitude for logistics and meal preparation:

> Daddy Days were my earliest opportunity to practice important life skills like planning, organization, and autonomy. Since it was my job to choose the activity and the menu, I had to start learning about logistics and trip preparation. I had to learn how to pack efficiently for an overnight backpacking excursion, consider the proximity of multiple activities, and select reasonable foods for the proposed activity. . . . I learned the importance of making a grocery list, and thoroughly enjoyed shopping for our day. Often, we included it as an activity. After all, it took both of us to choose a victory drink to share on the summit of the mountain we were climbing. We also started a tradition of trying exotic fruits, so scouring the produce section for the strangest looking one became a highlight.

Last year marked a first with Maria, as her one-year-old son, Andrew, joined us for a hike up a mountain on the New Hampshire "52 With a View" list. She suggested we tackle Smarts Mountain, the first three-thousand-foot peak as you hike along the Appalachian Trail from Dartmouth College in Hanover toward the White Mountains. We squeezed her Daddy Day in on a Saturday in August. She is still teaching and juggling life with Andrew, and I've got my usual busy list of activities. So, we made an executive decision that I would purchase and prepare lunch for the adults (remember, it would taste better to Maria if I made it) and she would prepare lunch for Andrew (half of which was brewed in her body).

Maria and I have very similar tastes. Even better, Maria was dubbed "Happy Heart" by her high school friends, so I could probably make PB&Js and bring Moxie, and she would be delighted. But to prepare for the adventure, I stopped at Market Basket and selected some fresh-baked Irish oatmeal bread, gorp (good old raisins and peanuts), tuna fish, apples

Grandson Andrew Schappler experiences his first hiking Daddy Day with Maria and Lito (short for Abuelito).

(it was late August, the perfect season), celery, peaches, and fresh baked maple-oatmeal raisin cookies. We were going to do a serious hike, so I knew we'd burn these calories.

Maria, Andrew, and I greatly enjoyed the drive up the western side of our state to an area that I had not explored. She carried Andrew. I carried food and drinks. Smarts is no Presidential Traverse, but it will certainly get your heart pumping if you hike at a decent pace. We naturally saved lunch as a reward in the firetower at the summit. If I dare say, those were a couple of the best tuna fish sandwiches I've ever had. Food was the easy part. The hard part was the victory drink selection—which is exactly what it sounds like: The beverage you enjoy after completing a strenuous adventure. This is probably not unique to me, but I do take it very seriously. Even the place you purchase your beverage is important. For instance, consider my 2021 Google review of Patch's Market in Bartlett, New Hampshire:

This place completely rocks. I ski Tuckerman a few times a year and this is my go-to for breakfast sandwiches and victory drinks. For those who have not had a fantastic experience here, I suggest a simple recipe:

1. *Walk in there with a huge smile on your face!*
2. *Greet them warmly and thank them for working during a pandemic!*
3. *Tip them generously for making awesome breakfast sandwiches! Simply said, it's gratitude. In my book, it works every time! Keep up the great work, Patch's!! I think you rock!*

Victory drinks are something that—in John Turner vernacular—are *super-wicked-good* to celebrate conquering a summit. In the case of skiing Tuckerman Ravine, we often just party at HoJos (the ranger cabin at the base of the ravine). Mine is often something silly and delicious like Nestle Strawberry Quik. Naked natural juices have become another favorite as I try to reach for more healthy choices. For the current adventure, Maria's only request was "IPA."

I spent more time debating that purchase than anything else at Market Basket. I was really hoping to find an Able Ebenezer Burn the Ships IPA for my history-loving (and teaching) daughter, but didn't find any—so I had to settle for a Tuckerman Brewing Fall Line. Friends that know me well will not be surprised that I've purchased more Tuckerman Brewing victory drinks than any other brand.

Whether Maria and I are driving to the mountain, hiking, or sipping IPAs on the summit, the conversations are always natural and enjoyable. We'll talk about everything from her mother, to her husband, to who to vote for in the next election. Hiking mountains as Daddy Days lends itself to deep and extended quality conversations—and I expect it's a tradition we'll never give up.

Ultimately, food selection is truly a critical ingredient of Daddy Days. If you are as lucky as I am, then your kids will participate in this with you, and if you're like me and food isn't a core part of your cultural background, it can—and should—still be a core part of your family traditions. Breaking bread is one of the best ways to share memories, hopes, fears, and love between parents and children, and even if the meal really just is a PB&J with Moxie, food is capable of bringing people closer.

Lesson 17: Nutrition. *Food is necessary, but it should also be fun. As part of Daddy Days, you can make food selection an important part of the day. You can encourage your kids to make healthy choices—or, in my case—they might push you to find something nourishing and healthy.*

PART 4

MARRIAGE

18 Unity

Renée and I met in 1990 at Saint Aidan's Church in Brookline, Massachusetts, the same parish where John F. Kennedy was baptized and raised as a child. The church is gone now, converted to high-end residential condos. Father Sal Ferigle, a charming and brilliant Spanish Opus Dei priest, was a notorious matchmaker. Watch the movie *The Jeweller's Shop*, based on a play written by Pope John Paul II, and you'll get a taste of how Father Sal worked. The priest in the movie similarly inspires young people to get together, date, and marry. Father Sal inspired many of us young adults to gather on Sunday mornings to discuss books or topics after Mass and then he'd encourage us to go get brunch together.

When someone at the brunch table one day started bashing Texas, Renée and I simultaneously and proudly defended the Lone Star State from opposite sides of the table and subsequently slapped a Texas-sized high five across the table—which I'm almost certain was the spark that first ignited between us. I recall Father Sal asking me when I was going to invite Renée and her CCD class (a Catholic religious education program) to join me and my CCD class to sing love songs for the elderly at a local nursing home. The guy was mischievous. What do you think happens when you sing love songs and there's a beautiful Cuban lady singing right along with you? Now, it didn't matter that Renée and I were dating others—the spark was growing to a flame.

Our first date was January 19, 1992. We went to a pro-life rally in Boston, where a bunch of protesters tried to interfere. Renée said later her heart melted when I gently stepped in front of her in a cowboy-style I'm-gonna-protect-you-babe move and made sure she was out of harm's way. We then walked over to Harvard Square and enjoyed Mexican food for dinner. I think we spent four hours at the dinner table. The poor server didn't turn our table that night.

She was a PhD student at Boston University living near Fenway Park, studying to earn her doctorate in Spanish literature. I was working in Waltham and had bought a tiny rundown farmhouse in Chelmsford. I couldn't stay away. I would drive into Boston after work just to take her on walks along the Charles River. Even if she was tied up with studies, I would bring her natural bouquets from the flora on my property. Other nights, she let me study with her at the library and we'd play footsies and I pretended to read.

I proposed March 19, eight weeks after our first date. I took her to Mass on the feast of Saint Joseph and then took her to Our Lady of Fatima Shrine in Brighton, where I painted graffiti on the snow with pink spray paint and proposed in an original poem read to her by candlelight. She quickly said yes, then came in Cuban-hot for a smooch during which I made the mistake of keeping the lit candle in my hand. When we embraced, I set her on fire. Her beautiful, long brown hair was going up in smoke. Fortunately, the fire was quickly contained and we only had to enjoy a new perfume for the rest of the evening. A fiery start to our engagement!

The walks to Boston Common, along Commonwealth Ave, and beside the Charles River continued. The passionate kisses grew stronger and longer. She departed in early June for Houston to prepare for our wedding, before which she visited Isle au Haut with me for Memorial Day weekend. I did not want to marry a woman that didn't understand my love affair with that island.

Now, Renée is a pistol, and I'm not a pushover. So, our attraction was accompanied by some disagreement as the wedding approached. The country boy wanted a reception on a Texas ranch. The city girl wanted a reception at Rice University (where she completed her master's degree). So, we made a deal: she would plan the wedding, I would plan the honeymoon. It's the way our marriage works well.

Renée got exactly the wedding she dreamed of at Annunciation Church in downtown Houston—the church where the marriage of her parents was consecrated. I got to scoop up my Cuban firecracker and carry her over the threshold, and I rented a convertible red Mustang as a getaway car. The reception at Rice University was classy. Renée was right. It was a beautiful, formal wedding and reception. And then it was my turn.

We exited the reception dragging a collection of cans and made onlookers cheer as we cruised through downtown and north to our getaway condo at April Sound on Lake Conroe. We spent just one night there. On day two, we hopped on a plane and flew to Phoenix. From there we rented a Chevy Corsica. It was no Mustang, but it didn't matter. We drove to a hilltop camping spot off a dirt road north of Jerome, Arizona, winding through the Black Mountains. We were running out of daylight but quickly pitched our tent amongst the cacti. I prepared lemon haddock over a campfire, and Renée enjoyed the first camping experience of her life—the first of many. We watched a lightning show in the distance as we sat next to a romantic campfire. The next morning, we bathed in a muddy-looking river. I assured my bride the water was clean. We even brushed our teeth in it before setting off for the Hualapai Indian Reservation. About a mile upstream, we saw a herd of cattle bathing in the water. I said nothing.

When we arrived at Hualapai Hilltop it was 105 degrees and my hundred-pound bride was given a fifteen-pound backpack to wear for the ten-mile hike down to the Havasu Falls campsite. The hiking book I had bought said it was a "strenuous" trek that typically took eight hours. Naturally dismissive, I said every hiking book exaggerates the difficulty of hikes and that we would knock it out in four.

Steam began blowing out Renée's ears less than a mile in. I recall her stomping down the trail crying that this was not her idea of a romantic honeymoon. There was not much I could do. We were committed, and I had packed over thirty pounds into my pack, so I could not easily take a load from her. To her credit, Renée settled in and we had a relatively quiet hike down to the Indian village. As dusk approached, the bats took interest in us.

We arrived at the village (a collection of modest dwellings with no power) well after dark and I offered to see if we could stay there, but Renée wanted to push on to our planned destination—the Havasu Falls campground, another two-plus miles downriver. We kept hiking. We were both exhausted from the tremendous heat and the backpacks.

It was pitch black. No moon. Our only light was a Mini Maglite powered by a limited supply of batteries. We largely navigated the trail by feel and the sound of the rushing river beside us. We had no idea how dangerous the trail was until we hiked out two days later. We arrived safely at the Havasu Falls campground after 1 A.M., set up the tent, and Renée was furious. I was exhausted and disappointed that she was not more excited about this adventure. I recall jumping in the chilly river that night to cool my jets.

We awoke to beautiful sunshine, warm temperatures, and the powerful sound of the mammoth Havasu Falls only two hundred feet from our tent. The Havasu River is the most astonishing electric blue-green water that I have ever seen, and the flowing water and falls create a tropical oasis in the bottom of the river valley as plants are treated to a near constant mist. Renée poked her beautiful face out of the tent and acknowledged with a big smile that we were in paradise.

I jumped into the frigid water and swam toward the waterfall. Renée dipped her toes at the edge and cheered me on. Now remember, this is 1992, safely before the internet made places like Havasu Falls popular. Today the State of Arizona website says: "Topping the bucket list of bucket lists, Havasu Falls in the Grand Canyon is one of the most sought after destinations in the world."

Renée and I were joined by perhaps ten other campers. We enjoyed the main falls for a while in the morning and then decided that we should hike downriver to the similarly spectacular Mooney Falls. We had the entire place to ourselves, and Renée's spirit of adventure had kicked in as she recognized we were blessed to be able to enjoy one of God's greatest creations.

We learned from others that the smartest time to hike was predawn. We did exactly that to exit the canyon. We packed up our camp at about 3 A.M. and had some moonlight to help us follow the trail. We hit Hualapai Hilltop at about 11 A.M., concluding what will go down as one of the most extraordinary adventures of my life. It was a serious test of our new marriage—one Renée and I passed together.

I always encourage engaged couples to take an adventure-filled honeymoon. Our honeymoon was not expensive, but it was a journey that strengthened our bond. Years later, when we started doing official Tarzan Days, we would reminisce about our honeymoon and how adventure intermingled with romance is an important part of keeping the flame alive in our marriage. Even more, learning how to survive adventures like this with your spouse is great preparation for parenthood. Raising children is a journey all on its own—and it's one best done with someone you count on to be by your side even when the trail leaves you exhausted.

Lesson 18: Unity. *If you want a strong relationship with your children, start with a loving relationship with your wife. Having an adventure partner in your life with whom you can overcome challenges will better equip you to give your best to your children. Fatherhood is not an isolated experience. Often, the best fathers first find strength in a marriage.*

Devotion

I often tease my bride that the most developed bone in her body is her jealous bone. It didn't take too many years of me treating the kids to Daddy Days before Renée suggested it would be nice if I gave *her* something similar for Christmas. So, we started our own tradition. Here's how Renée described it recently:

> When John started Daddy Days with our children, I felt somewhat left out, so I suggested we have some time away for just the two of us. We called that time Tarzan Days because like Tarzan, my husband is a wild outdoorsman and like Jane, I'm more of a city girl.

It's true. I run around whenever possible barefoot (including at work), I shower outside every day from Easter through Halloween, and my comfort zone has always been in the wilderness. Renée, on the other hand, is much more like Jane—opting for the comforts of home.

The same rules I use with the kids apply: Renée gets a day with me in which she can pick the activity. One year, Renée decided we'd go whale watching (which, to be clear, was *not* my idea of a good time). I said yes and bought us tickets on one of the boats out of Rye Harbor. It didn't take long before Renée was feeling seasick. That, combined with rain showers and pretty lame whale sightings (I don't think we got closer than a quarter mile to a breach!), didn't make for a particularly fun outing, especially for Renée.

But, as part of Renée's Tarzan Day, we rented a room at a bed and breakfast in Ogunquit. And thankfully I'd strapped the canoe onto our vehicle before we left home. So, the next day, we attended church in the nearby village—where one of Renée's coworker's students was now pastor—and we dropped the canoe into the York River for a good paddle. Renée reflected later that our canoe paddle was her favorite activity of her Tarzan Day. It always feels like a small victory when my suggested activity ends up being the favorite.

Kayaking together at Wentworth-Coolidge Mansion (Portsmouth, NH) on Renée's Tarzan Day.

One of our best Tarzan Days was a weekend in Boston. After all, it's where we first met and dated. We splurged on a single night at the Omni Parker House. It was fun to revisit the little restaurant in Fenway where I first suggested to my girlfriend that we sit on the same side of a booth. Renée at first thought it was awkward, but quickly decided that it was rather romantic, and we've maintained that tradition now for thirty-two years. Restaurant hosts often smile when they set the places opposite in a booth, and we ask them permission to sit together on one side. During our Tarzan weekend in Boston, we walked along the Charles, visited Boston Common, returned to Our Lady's Guilt House (my name for Our Lady's Guild House, where she lived when I was courting her). It was a relatively simple weekend, but among the most special we've shared.

If you're looking for ideas to share time with your wife, steal this one: Take her back to where you courted her. Revisit those places. Propose to her again where you originally proposed (this time remember to take a knee and avoid lighting her on fire). Talk to her. No, that's not it, *listen* to her! Pay attention. Be patient. Tease her. Hold her hand. Walk at her speed. Look into her eyes. Tell her that you love her. Kiss her with the same passion that you did when you were dating. Treat her like a lady.

A second proposal of marriage on a Tarzan Day—nineteen years into our marriage.

Date your mate. That's pretty standard marriage advice, right? Renée and I have benefited from Nicky and Sila Lee's The Marriage Course over the years. It's a program that provides a structured venue for all couples to improve their marriage. We have taken the course at least four times—and if you're looking for help keeping your marriage together, it's worth exploring. If your relationship is anything like ours, you've probably found that a quick dinner out is not always a recipe for a perfect date.

We both really like how the Marriage Course is structured, normally presented in seven date nights, one per week. The program guides you to deep conversations about difficult topics (conflict, forgiveness, family, sex, etc.). As most parents with adult children can probably relate to, there are myriad opportunities for conflict as you raise children: what to feed them, when and how to comfort them, how to handle the school bully, what movies to watch, when to set their curfew. The course has taught us how to work together better, and it's simply normal that extended times together also often lend themselves to important conversations. Even when we felt totally under water, using the tools of the Marriage Course helped us swim back to the surface together and enjoy fresh air.

Renée and I began Tarzan Days twelve years into our marriage. By then, we had three kids: Maria was ten, Carlos was six, and Cecilia was four. Fortunately, we had family and friends who agreed to take care of them when we went on these (generally) weekend-long adventures. A few of the early Tarzan Day certificates came with a suggested budget limit of three hundred dollars. Despite this, we still have had great times. Our very first Tarzan Day was an escape to Newport, Rhode Island, to explore the mansions. It sounds expensive, but we drove down, bicycled around, enjoyed the beach, and then stayed at a B&B. We finished the weekend at least close to our budget.

The difference between a Tarzan Day and a date is simple: quality time. It's pretty easy to go out on a date Friday night, enjoy dinner, and return home. Spending a whole weekend together demands (well, if you take this seriously) that you really get to know your mate again. On our third year of Tarzan Days, we left our kids with my sister Sue and brother-in-law Stewart at their home in Massachusetts and then shot back to our own home for a staycation. Our house was beautiful, and it was great fun to enjoy it for two nights without kids. It was also an economical choice and a preview of what empty nesting would bring years later.

Perhaps the opposite of a staycation: Lunch at the 21 Club in New York City.

Renée and I are currently experiencing the emotional roller coaster associated with our kids having left home. Like most parents, our lives were very kid-centric for many years. Today, our oldest, Maria, is happily married and lives just thirty minutes from our home with our grandson. That gives us lots of opportunity to spend time with her and her growing family. Somehow, our younger children—Carlos and Cecilia—now reside in Texas. So, it's become much harder to see them as much as we would like. This is particularly difficult for Renée as she is now retired and no longer has the distraction of full-time employment.

I'm convinced that spending Tarzan Days together each year was helpful practice, reminding us of the joy of adventuring together and simply enjoying each other's company. Naturally, with two of our children out of state, Renée and I travel more together for family visits. And, as always, good adventures keep us pleasantly distracted. It's easy to get wound up about expenses and all the difficulties in life—but it's often necessary to let go and simply enjoy each other's company. It's also a reminder that your marriage is the bedrock of your family's foundation. Renée has communicated this to me, too. Recently, she reflected on the concept:

> Tarzan Days with my husband have opened "a whole new world"—as the song from *Aladdin* goes. Like Princess Jasmine, I trusted and have enjoyed my carpet ride for over thirty years now. I hope we have many more years of activities together ahead. Life with Tarzan has opened up new horizons and forced me to become more extroverted than I ever imagined. It is what my husband said to me when we were dating and when we were first married: "We don't watch movies. We make them." It is true. We continue to make movies as empty nesters and as grandparents.

Well, it's not a carpet, but our tandem mountain bike, Tango (because it takes two to Tango) has been a source of lots of fun—including on the causeway in Lake Champlain near Burlington, Vermont.

Aside from the grace of God, commitment is the most important ingredient in a successful marriage. I am not an easy person to be married to. I know this. I am tremendously overcommitted with activities and Renée reminds me that she too often takes a backseat to other priorities. I am fortunate that she is completely committed to our marriage, and I do often remind her that I am also completely committed. Scheduling one-on-one time every year to break away (for more than a weekly date) from life's many obligations is a crucial part of the formula to making our marriage work.

Lesson 19: Devotion. *My uncle John Spurk taught me about the three types of love: Filial, agape, and eros. Eros is the spark in a relationship. It's the easiest to kindle and the quickest to snuff out. Be deliberate in setting up adventures that will help strike that match again. It's good for you, good for your wife, and good for your children to see that their parents are still in love.*

Commitment

Renée and I have often returned to Quebec, both the city and province, to rekindle our love. The walled city, which feels like it could easily be in France, is quaint and full of life—an ideal place for romantic strolls. The surrounding province is peaceful, and lush, and an easy place to lose the crowds. As our 2023 Tarzan Day was approaching, Renée suggested returning to the Abbaye de Saint-Benoît-du-Lac, where she'd previously done a retreat. Renée was nourished for decades by the Benedictine monks at Saint Anselm College, where she worked for over twenty-five years, and she knew she would be similarly inspired by this Benedictine community near Magog.

We agreed our adventure would begin with a Mass there. We enjoyed an early morning drive from New Hampshire and arrived in time for a service that was performed in French. We then bought a pile of cheese, wine, and other goodies from the monastery gift shop and enjoyed a picnic on the grounds. This was my speed: good food, outdoors, and the top of a hill with my beautiful bride.

We continued into Magog and found our lodging, which was an easy walk to town. We visited a distillery and strolled along the waterfront park. Renée chose the dinner venue, Au Comptoir MarCel, which was perhaps the best restaurant experience we've ever had. The following morning, we did a good power walk at Marais de la Rivière-aux-Cerises. If you like boardwalks, this one is outstanding, featuring marshlands, bird-watching, and a nature center with a cute café. This Tarzan Day was no Havasu Falls adventure, but it was a pleasant blend of fresh air, new experiences, and special time away together. Part of what I believe makes for the best adventures is no (or very little) agenda and deadlines. Our Magog trip was a good example. We were both relaxed and enjoyed the intimate time together.

Renée convinced me a few years ago to take her to a Jane Austen–inspired bed and breakfast in Vermont for one of her Tarzan Days. I said yes on the condition that we would also take along our tandem mountain bike to explore Vermont's Lamoille Valley Rail Trail. It was a perfect compromise: she enjoyed the classy lodging and dining, while I got my zoomies out by burning calories on the rail trail. The tandem mountain bike has been a marriage saver for me because I can get as much exercise as I desire without leaving Renée in the dust. She also was surprised on that trip to see me chill and enjoy soaking in a clawfoot tub—something that I'm not likely to do at home where there are Christmas trees to prune and fire calls to respond to.

That weekend was such a delight for Renée that she recently challenged me to a full Jane Austen character weekend at the same place. Her sales pitch included me playing the delightful Mr. Bingley from *Pride and Prejudice*, and she would play the lovely and compliant Miss Jane Bennet (well, actually, Mrs. Bingley since we were to share a bedchamber). She also promised that she would be as in love with me as Jane was of Charles Bingley—a part she played quite well. In a reflection she shared for this book, Renée thought I played my role well, too.

> John was an excellent Charles Bingley. He even watched both *Pride and Prejudice* movies that we own before we did the character weekend and had his hairdresser give him some kind of hairspray to fluff up his hair. He acted very much like Charles Bingley. He didn't complain once and he just did everything. He was amicable and cheerful. Despite being the only man there, he behaved naturally and was wonderfully entertaining, gracious, and

gentlemanly to all. I was very proud of him and I had an excellent time. We went on a carriage ride, played croquet with the group, learned to play the card game whist, and enjoyed Regency period dancing.

Bed and Breakfast character weekend—Mr. and Mrs. Charles Bingley.

It's true that I embraced my character, and dutifully, as well as the theme of the weekend. But it was also a serious test of my patience. After all, my natural state of being has little in common with the English gentry of the eighteenth and nineteenth centuries. And there were some elements of the weekend that really tested me. Our host, for instance, was a serial micro-manager. When we were line dancing, the house was steamy with no air conditioning. Everyone was sweating profusely. I was reprimanded when I suggested opening doors and windows to allow some cool night air to pass through (the owner's concern was that a bat—yes, a *bat*—might enter the house).

But in hindsight, I was grateful that Renée had challenged me to play Mr. Bingley as I was greatly inspired to control that stallion within me and simply be cheerful and amicable. My patience was tested hard, but Renée said that I passed. It might not have been a weekend I dreamt up, but part of being committed to a relationship is doing things *for* other people—and doing them with a smile on your face.

Lesson 20: Commitment. *It's important to remind your spouse that you love and are committed to them by the way you practice patience. Sometimes, you just need to work together and not complain. It's not unlike riding a tandem bicycle with your wife—a wonderful way to practice the art of working together. It takes patience for both of you, and it won't work if you're not both committed to the challenge. By modeling patience in your marriage, you're also setting an important example for your children. It will help them learn to control their temper and emotions—an essential life skill.*

PART 5

EVOLUTION

Days as Gifts

When my kids were young, my niece Julie Andrasik was the recipient of what I would call Uncle John gift days—and she was a darn tough adventure companion with our family, serving in some ways as an older sister to my kids. Despite growing up in Kentucky and Ohio, she was often present as we ascended mountains throughout New England (her son, Zach, is now a frequent companion on these treks). Julie, along with her brother, helped define a concept that would become known in our family as the "Psycho Hiko." These hikes, as you likely have gathered over the course of this book, tend to be unpredictable. Among the other criteria:

1. The schedule is not optional. We're going on this adventure no matter what the meteorologist says; we may or *may not* adjust our agenda based on the weather.

2. There is no advanced plan. We will discuss the hike options the night before our adventure at the Turner Watering Hole (our kitchen).

3. The adventure will be challenging. They are misogi-like endeavors.

4. The participants may make the whole experience extra challenging.

A memorable Psycho Hiko came in 2010 on Mount Katahdin—Maine's tallest peak at 5,269 feet—and its legendary, treacherous Knife

Edge Trail. At various points along the ridge, the trail is only three feet wide with fifteen-hundred-foot sheer drops on either side. For this adventure, I was joined by Maria and Julie's sister, Courtney, as well as two other cousins, Brielle and Kateri. I had summitted Katahdin several times before this trek, but the weather handed to these ladies was the worst I've seen: Cold, wind-driven rain, poor visibility. These conditions chill you to the bone and result in a misogi-like experience.

I'm amazed to this day that they were willing to hike the entire Knife Edge Trail, which is scary to climb in dry and clear conditions. Add rain, wind, and poor visibility and it's downright nerve-wracking. I don't recall encountering any other hikers on the entire Knife Edge Trail that day. I was very fortunate that despite the scary conditions, my nieces and daughter completed the scramble. When we got back to our campsite, I worked hard to take care of them.

This hike was not only a test of our grit and an opportunity for us to grow, it was also an example of the Daddy Days concept extrapolated to include more of the family. While the practice began—and in many cases remains—as one-on-one adventures with my immediate family, I have found great joy over the years including others when the opportunity arises.

My daughter Maria married a fantastic person in John Schappler. I gave him his first formal Daddy Day certificate when they were engaged, and he suggested that we golf together at the Jamestown Golf Course in Rhode Island (they were living and working in that state at the time). It was a blast, and it helped grow a relationship with a soon-to-be member of my family—a perfect example of why Daddy Days are so special, an opportunity for one-on-one time when we get to have conversations at all levels.

This started a tradition, and now John's annual certificate is no longer a Daddy Day—it's a "Golf with JT Day"—and of the many certificates I give each year, he's often the first to cash his in. As of April 2024, John was married five years to Maria, had been a dad himself for a year, and was well on his way to a radical career swap from high school teacher to firefighter. Spending time with him as he navigated life transitions has been a joy—and I'm proud of the man he's become. As this book was taking shape, I asked him to reflect on the one-on-one time we have shared over the years. I was struck by how he captured the spirit of Golf Days:

> We are far from professional, but that's not what it's about out there. We may drink a few more beers than we make pars, but that's the fun of it . . . it's about making memories that will last a lifetime, and starting traditions that can be looked forward to each year. Daddy Days, which for me have become Golf Days, have given me a chance to get to know John in a way that I would suspect not all people have with their in-laws. It gives us a chance to talk about life, to joke around, and to have fun. A chance to let go of stress and commitments, and give your attention fully to someone else. . . . Our golf days are, in a way, a forced relaxation. Where we don't have to worry about the stresses of life. Where we can shank the ball into the woods and laugh about it. When at the end of the day it is just two people having a good time, enjoying the outdoors, and sipping on some IPAs. . . . The beauty of the gift is that John isn't giving a tangible object that will one day become obsolete. He's giving time and memories to a person he cares about. It is my opinion that time is the most valuable thing that you can give to a person. The time I can give to my own son is one of the most important things in the world to me. I live my life every day trying to remember that simple fact.

John Schappler is not the only extension of my family now receiving gifts. Carlos recently brought a young woman into our lives that Renée and I both adore. After a few years bushwhacking across the country, Carlos landed in Houston, Texas (well, that's where his jalopy broke down). He was broke. His timing was fortuitous as Renée's cousin, Juan,

John Schappler's first "Golf Day"—Awesome annual father-son-in-law tradition.

was in need of carpenters. Carlos had developed carpentry skills framing houses here in New Hampshire, and thus had the right resume to help with finish carpentry at the beautiful Lanier Theological Library just outside of Houston.

Carlos is handsome and charming, so it was no surprise that he soon met a lovely and equally kind woman named Halli. They had just started dating when Carlos had made a visit to New Hampshire for a rugged backpacking Daddy Day adventure in the White Mountains (Carlos summited two Four-thousand Footers barefoot!). So, when we started discussing his Daddy Day in 2024, Halli got the invitation to join us for a "real" hike in the northeast.

One of the most popular hikes for serious mountaineers in New Hampshire is the Presidential Traverse Trail—more than eighteen granite miles encompassing nearly a dozen peaks, depending on the route you take. The plans were laid early in the year and we scored a reservation for the famous AMC Lake of the Clouds Hut on Mount Washington, the natural midpoint overnight rest for those tackling the traverse. To prepare, Halli sent me a copy of Michael Easter's *Comfort Crisis*—a rallying cry for our adventure.

We were gifted a banner first day. We started our ascent of Mount Madison at about 8:30 A.M. and were all quickly reminded of why fellow hikers find this one to be a butt-kicker. The weather was spectacular, but Halli's body was not feeling perfect. At the Madison Hut, we decided to bypass the extra climb up to the Madison summit and hike on to Mount Adams. While Halli quietly soaked in the sites and carefully placed every foot, the eleven-year-old chatterbox Zach (my niece Julie's son) kept us entertained with his thoughts about, well, everything!

Carlos and Halli were responsible for food selection, and thus we enjoyed kombucha tea victory drinks on the summit of Mount Adams. Shortly after our Adams lunch, the ever kind and equally rugged Carlos volunteered to add Halli's pack to his own (he literally just hung hers from his) to help her make it to our destination. We bypassed the summits of Mount Jefferson, Mount Clay, and Mount Washington, and once we were in sight of the hut, Zach and I picked up the pace, both dropping our gear and beelining into one of the lakes as Carlos and Halli enjoyed the approaching sunset.

Maria and John, who had summited Mount Washington the same day, kindly delivered drinks for an evening refreshment and sustenance for our second day on the trail. We enjoyed a few hands of gin rummy and settled in pretty early to our busy and stuffy bunk room. The rain started during the night. After all, it would not be one of my adventures without some challenging weather. Maria and John, a former meteorologist, made the educated move and hiked down the same day.

In the morning, we summited Mount Monroe in light rain. The clouds and spotty precipitation continued throughout the day, but the visibility was decent—making the scenery iconic of the White Mountains with fir trees, rocky summits, and rays of sun poking through the ever-shifting cloud layer. We hiked around Mount Eisenhower and summited Mount Pierce before descending to our car. We wouldn't set any records, but we concluded the adventure with no significant injuries. Most importantly, we all took home a tremendous memory of doing this challenging hike together. And, by including more people into the adventure, I was able to develop deeper bonds with my son, his fiancée, and my grandnephew.

Summit of Mount Adams, New Hampshire with Zach, Halli, and Carlos—Presidential Traverse.

I didn't know it at the time, but as we hiked those miles, Carlos was reflecting on how his cousin was benefitting from the concept. Later, he shared with me that on this journey he began thinking about how he could pass the Daddy Days tradition on to a new generation.

> "This experience gave me a look into the other side of Daddy Days. I was now able to enrich the experience for my cousin and show him the joy of the great outdoors. During this adventure

> I reflected on the idea that one day, it will be me taking my children out into the wilderness. I look forward to the chance to pass on some of the wisdom my father has shared with me. I am forever grateful for the time my dad has spent with me. I will cherish these memories forever.

I'm a firm believer that time is one our greatest gifts, and over the years it's one I've shared even beyond my immediate and extended family. I have been fortunate to sponsor a fair number of young men to be confirmed in the Catholic faith. To be confirmed marks a serious commitment in a person's faith life; it's the moment in which they *choose* to be a full member of the Church and, in doing so, confirm the vows made at baptism. It's one of the three sacraments of initiation (along with baptism and first communion), but it is the first sacrament in which the decision rests with the individual rather than with the parents. In essence, confirmation represents a decision to continue being Catholic.

Tom Dahlberg, the son of a close friend of mine, was one of many who asked if I would serve as his sponsor. I understand the gravity of the sacrament, and I consider it a great honor to guide young people through it. And, as such, I also offer a gift to those young people—my favorite being a dedicated day, not unlike the Daddy Days concept. It's the same deal: they pick an adventure and we go after it together.

At the time, Tom wanted to see New York City, so we loaded up mountain bikes, drove to the city, and rode the Hudson River Waterfront Greenway before visiting Saint Patrick's Cathedral, the roof deck of the Empire State Building and Ground Zero. We also rode *The Beast*, a large open speedboat that soaks its passengers by chasing waves on the Hudson River. We even jumped in for a quick swim under the George Washington Bridge before driving back to New Hampshire—all in one day.

The concept of Daddy Days can play out in countless relationships in our lives, some which may be unexpected. I was about thirty years old when a young man named Derek Russell knocked on the front door of my business, which at the time was called Criterium-Turner Engineers. He told me he was a structural engineering student at the University of New Hampshire and that he was seeking a summer internship. I admired his initiative—and after a short conversation I offered him a job. He quickly became one of my family's favorite tagalongs on adventures as we would sail, hike, and explore the natural wonder of our home state. Though he wasn't my biological kin, I was able to share the gift of time with him nonetheless.

People like Derek who I've worked with over many decades helped me learn that team building often requires bonding experiences beyond the parameters of a job site. Today, the Team Engineering staff still enjoy what we call Quarterly Fun Days in which we leave the office and engage in activities together. These have included horseback riding, visits to the Museum of Fine Arts in Boston, glass blowing, downhill skiing, and pottery making. These outings are regularly scheduled ways for us to better understand each other and grow as a team.

Goffstown, New Hampshire, where Renée and I lived from 1993 until 2000, is home to two beautiful, perky peaks nearly identical in height (the south summit is 1,321 feet; the north is 1,324) and aptly named the Uncanoonucs (a Native American word meaning "woman's breasts.") Both mountains have been preserved for recreation and are riddled with hiking trails. Over the years, I've explored these mountains extensively—mostly solo, but more recently, I've become fond of challenging others to join me. It has become the Wednesday morning routine in my life, and I have a few regular companions who are willing to show up at 7 A.M. and hit the trail. We typically are up and down the south peak in less than an hour, after which I'll swim in Mountain Base Pond before heading off to work.

During the winter months, we switch to uphill skiing, or skinning, at Pat's Peak in Henniker, New Hampshire. It's a craze I've become fairly addicted to, and thankfully it's one that has allowed me to connect with friends and coworkers on a deeper level as we shuffle our skis up the 770 vertical feet of modest terrain. I am typically the oldest member of our group—often twice the age of other participants—and I find great joy in listening to the thoughts, feelings, and fears of the younger generation. It reminds me of the conversations I have with my own children. And they humor me with patience as I share about my latest challenge. Mornings like this are a blessing—and a tremendous use of time.

Lesson 21: Days as Gifts. *I've always been grateful for my sailing mentor, Pat O'Connell. He didn't have a son but treated me like one. He was generous with his time and shared his joy of sailing. This was a huge inspiration for my own life. Perhaps you don't have a son. Perhaps you share dreams with a niece, nephew, or in-law. Share your time and things you love with others! We spend more of our waking time at work than anywhere else. Introduce the gift of time to your workplace. Build relationships with your workplace team by scheduling days to learn together. Spend time listening to coworkers. Encourage them.*

Affirmation

If decades of parenting has made anything clear, it's that we will not understand every decision our children make—and that it's *okay.* Every choice a child makes offers an opportunity for a parent to understand them on a deeper level and support them, even if it's hard to grapple with in the moment.

I have spent countless hours reflecting on the role of fathers in the lives of children, and one of the best sources of wisdom I've found on the subject comes from Fr. Dave Pivonka, the president of Franciscan University of Steubenville. His recent series, *My father's Father,* explores the urgent crisis of fatherlessness in modern society and presents viewers a spiritual pathway to connecting with God and becoming better fathers themselves. "The starting place with God the Father is actually our earthly father," Pivonka says. "The deepest desire of every human heart is to be seen. And not just in a vague sense, but to be seen by a father."

One of my family's favorite movies is *Cool Runnings,* the 1993 film depicting the Jamaican bobsled team's improbable efforts at the 1988 Winter Olympics. At one point in the film, a character named Junior struggles with his dad's disapproval of his decision to "slide down a bunch of ice on his backside." Eventually, one of his teammates tells him to look in the mirror and asks him what he sees. When Junior demurs, his teammate tells him what he *should* see: "Pride. Power. And a bad ass mother who don't take no crap off nobody."

Carlos was a little boy when we first started watching *Cool Runnings* as a family. I would stand him on top of our bathroom sink and ask him what he saw in the mirror. He would timidly answer, "A boy." I would challenge him to see "Pride. Power. And a bad ass mother who don't take no crap off nobody!" I don't think Carlos saw that for years—and perhaps still doesn't today. However, he always knew what I saw. I saw my incredible son—earning his belts in karate, giving it his all on the basketball court, ripping up the soccer field with his teammates, running like a gazelle at track and cross country, dominating the lacrosse field. I was always proud of his wonderful mix of skill and sportsmanship. I understood then what Pivonka teaches today: Carlos needed to be *seen* by his father.

It was easy to be a raving fan of Carlos the boy and student. He was handsome, talented, and kind. He could win in sports and could simultaneously be recognized for sportsmanship. Children desperately need the approval of their fathers and this came easy to me when he was young. But when Carlos grew older, like many, his journey and mission became unclear. And, if I'm being candid, it was harder for me to approve of what I saw as an unemployed skateboarder who found thrill in taunting City Hall. That didn't stop me from loving him.

I always felt a deep tenderness for my son, and even in his days of minimal ambition I consistently cared for him. Whether it was hitchhiking or dropping out of college, Carlos always knew that he had my support. This is not to say that I gave Carlos a free ride. I recall that he had about a thousand dollars in his bank account when he started hitchhiking around Europe. With three weeks to go prior to his return flight, his balance was down to zero. Renée and I agreed that we would give him an early Christmas gift that year: five hundred dollars to buy some food so he wouldn't starve.

Maria and Cecilia have experienced the same commitment and joyful fatherly approval from me. I'm by no means claiming perfection, but I worked hard over the years to show up and be present at their important events. And they made it easy for me to be present for and proud of them.

There were ballet performances, plays, soccer and basketball games. I was always delighted to see how different each of my children was—especially when they would surprise me.

For instance, Cecilia had been studying criminal justice and psychology and many in our family thought she would find her way into law enforcement as a detective or special agent. But when she told us she was shifting gears to become an ABA (applied behavior analysis) therapist serving those with autism, I celebrated her decision. I needed to show her that I approved and that I would be proud of her no matter what she chose to do professionally.

Relationships like these are built over years, not days. I won't claim that Daddy Days are the silver bullet to being a good father. Of course one day a year with a child won't create a great relationship unless these moments are part of daily commitment to show love and affirm them. But by committing to regular, serious, and very focused adventures and activities that promote deep conversation and one-on-one time with your children, you are given extraordinary opportunities to express your complete approval to your children. As Maria recently told me: "The consistency of a gift of time every year was a constant reminder that I was loved and that I mattered."

I learned this lesson both from my earthly father as well as our heavenly Father—and I firmly believe these relationships are essential for bringing joy to the world. A true father's love is selfless, unconditional, sacrificial, and everlasting. This is exactly how God loves us. He sees us and affirms us—and He approves.

Lesson 22: Affirmation. *Affirm your children and try to love them as God would. In your words and actions, remind them that you love them for who they are, not for who you want them to be. Remind them that God wants us to experience heaven on earth—not just in the afterlife. Daddy Days can be utilized to share joy in life as God wants us to experience.*

23 Role Reversal

It's hard to know exactly when it happens, but as you and your children age, the relationship you share begins to change. Eventually, they start teaching the lessons, guiding the adventures, selecting the food, and pushing you beyond your comfort zone in a way that *you* once did for them. Each of my children have reminded me of this in recent years.

With Cecilia, it was perhaps a weekend trip I took to visit her while she was living in Virginia. She planned an intense schedule and had me ride public transportation, visit museums, attend a dog show, and experience an escape room with her. These activities were very much inspired by her and it was really rewarding to have Cecilia lead the adventure.

With Maria, the nudge outside of my comfort zone recently was not on her Daddy Day. Rather, it was to host two foreign exchange students from Spain. It would have been easier to decline hosting Olivia and Claudia last September, but Maria explained to us that these students really needed a host family. Naturally, Renée and I worked hard to make their visit to America as rewarding as possible. We attended a football game with them and brought them to a variety of activities. I even took them sailing. Ultimately, I'm very grateful that our daughter challenged us to share our home and a bit of our life with these two young ladies.

Perhaps the most serious example came in 2024 when Carlos suggested that for his 2025 Daddy Day we should run the Big Bend Ultra Trail Race near the Mexican border in southwest Texas. Big Bend is one of the country's largest and least-visited national parks featuring nearly a million acres of jagged mountains, desert plains, and cactus-dotted foothills. The Big Bend Ultra was created in 2004 and today features five distances: 10k, 20k, 30k, 50k, and 50 miles. Carlos had already committed to running the 50k, a 31.1 mile course on hiking trails through an arid landscape that will make your skin and lips crack. If the heat and high elevation aren't enough, the rocks, ruts, dust, and soft sand only make the course more daunting.

When he first told me about it, all the normal objections entered my brain: I can't afford it. And it's too much time away from my wife, work, and other responsibilities. But then I realized, to quote the famous Nike slogan, sometimes you need to *Just Do It.* It's a lesson I first learned from my own father, who was a master at making things happen that didn't seem possible. And in this case, my son was only asking me for a few days of my time. Plus, I was awfully proud of him and his fiancée, Halli, who was helping him kick cigarettes and take up running again. Carlos had also just reread *Born To Run,* and to entice me into this race he and Halli sent me a copy. I got the message. Challenge accepted.

Though I have run periodically throughout my life, it's never been my favorite form of cardio workout. In some ways, it's like hunting: I'll do it if someone really wants me to, but it isn't going to be my preferred activity. In this case, I had no choice: It was time to get my fifty-eight-year-old body back into shape for running—something I hadn't done regularly in decades. Given my busy life, a dislocated hip injury from fifteen years ago, and general aging, I signed up for the 10k event and Halli agreed to join me. Having a race date on the calendar inspired me to run at least twice a week and ruck (walking while carrying weight on my back) once a week. Having Carlos and Halli as accountability partners was crucial to my weekly motivation.

They suggested we were in this together—not just for the run but also for the experience of exploring Big Bend National Park together. They found an eclectic place to stay, a small cabin in the Terlingua Ranch area just northwest of the park and about an hour from where the January race would take place. Renée and I flew together into Houston and were treated to dinner at Halli's grandparents' home—a special occasion to get to know Carlos's, future in-laws. Renée stayed with extended family in Houston while Carlos, Halli, and I made the nearly ten-hour drive out to the west side of the park. Two of their friends joined us for the journey.

Tarantula Ranch, the name of the cabin, was equal parts remote and scenic. As we bumped our way down a two-mile Jeep road, I told myself the deep tissue massage I was getting from the seat would be good for my legs when the race began. We did a short hike the first day we were there, and Carlos and I did a "warmup" run together up a steep hill. It was grueling. Trying to keep up with Carlos caused me to worry about my fate in the race. Later that afternoon, we made our way to the U.S.–Mexico border where Halli had arranged an engagement photoshoot in Saint Elena Canyon (Carlos had proposed to Halli atop Mount Washington the prior fall), a place where the Rio Grande slows to a trickle and cliff walls make crossing the border an impossibility.

The next morning, Carlos's race began at 7 A.M., so Halli and I watched his start before seeking warmth in the car. Temperatures were still in the thirties when my 10k race began two hours later. When I stepped into the starting corral, I was wearing a *Certified Psycho* t-shirt (a gift from Carlos and Halli), shorts, and leather work gloves. A sight to behold. Back when I raced cross country skiing, I always chose to start at the rear of the pack. I've never sought first place, and I don't like to adventure alone. I took the same strategy this time. After picking off the slower crowd, the racers were stretching out.

As I approached the mid-way point, I spotted a runner that looked like my real pacer. I stalked the guy twenty to thirty yards back for most of the second half of the race. He started pulling away at the 9k point, but then suddenly dropped to a walk. I quickly caught up and challenged him to cross the finish line together running with me as he had inspired me for much of the race. We did just that and it was enough to put me second for my age group. Halli and I regrouped at the finish line and waited for Carlos to come into view—which he did at around noon. He, too, placed second in his age group.

After retreating to the cabin, we wound down with a hearty meal, a soak in the hot tub, and a few hands of cards. The next morning, we were right back at it, climbing Emery Peak, the highest mountain in Big Bend National Park. As we strode up manmade steps and later scrambled up to the highest pinnacle, I realized that in many ways I was now following in the footsteps of my son and his partner. A light wind was blowing, the sky was joyously blue, and as I stared out across the panoramas of the park and out across the mountains of Mexico, it dawned on me that I was receiving the gift this time around. Carlos inspired me to race. He booked the lodging. He planned the itinerary. Our roles had reversed. All I had to do was say yes.

A gift from Halli and Carlos to me—running in the Big Bend Ultra.

The older I get, the more these days feel like a gift from my children and loved ones to me. Their schedules are getting busier and more complicated than mine. Their resources are more limited. Their vacation times are shorter. I don't think that I'll ever stop "giving" these days, but I'll also never stop reminding myself that it is equally a gift from them that they say "yes" and choose to give me the gift of their time, company, and inspiration to see and do great things together.

Lesson 23: Role Reversal. *Evangelize those around you by your word and, more important, by your actions. Remind them that God wants us to experience heaven on earth—not just in the afterlife. I know that my #1 job in life is to get my own tail and then to help my wife and children get into heaven. Daddy and Gift Days can be utilized to share joy in life as God wants us to experience. If you are blessed as I have been, your children and loved ones will reward you with a willingness to share their life, time, and loved ones with you!*

Afterword by John Turner

There's an old quote from author Jerry Minchey: "Some people make things happen, some people watch things happen, and some people wonder what happened." My youngest daughter Cecilia and I both like to *make* things happen—and watching her grow, and make things happen for herself, has always inspired me. I owe her credit, too, because as I reflect back on how this book came to be, it was in conversation with Cecilia that the idea for this book first materialized.

I began writing *Daddy Days* on a Sunday night in the fall of 2023. I was sitting in Dulles International Airport in Virginia, and if all went well, I'd make it home to Amherst, New Hampshire, at about 2 A.M. The next day, I would be exhausted, but it would be well worth the memories I made with Cecilia on her annual Daddy Day. That weekend had started two days prior with an early flight out of Boston. When I arrived in Virginia, Cecilia, a determined organizer, had given me detailed instructions on how to take public transportation from the airport to her place in Herndon. I have rural sensibilities, so I generally prefer my own wheels to public transportation, but I must admit the train was easy and convenient, a worry-free start to a weekend-long adventure.

There was no rest for the weary. Just as I arrived, we turned around and took the same train into Washington, DC, to visit the Air and Space Museum. The place is extraordinary, but Ceci and I both have limited attention spans for museums, so we moved through it quickly. We returned to Herndon, walked her dog, Tango, and then hit a classy market where I saw my first grocery-cart-escalator (country boy goes to the city!) and bought a pile of groceries and headed back to her place. Over dinner, we talked about her professional journey from New Hampshire to

Virginia, and how the reality of her employment there was very different from the expectation she was given. We also talked about how Daddy Days have helped us create so many memories together despite our very different natural interests.

On Saturday morning, we explored Herndon, enjoyed fresh baked goods for breakfast, and then headed to an escape room where we worked together to free ourselves from a multiroom murder mystery with a fair bit of horror mixed in. I recall that one of us had to stand up inside a fireplace as though we were going up the chimney. If that weren't creepy enough, another point in the lab required us to stick our hands into a garbage disposal, which naturally made it turn on—though it did not mangle any fingers. It was a challenging, scary, and gratifying experience with Cecilia, who loves all things mystery.

As we continued our weekend together—we went apple picking, we shared more meals, and I even watched Cecilia and her poodle compete at a dog show—I kept reflecting on the meaning of Daddy Days and the lessons my family had learned from the tradition. By the end of the weekend, the seed of an idea was sprouting. At the airport, readying to go home, my brain was racing. I reflected about the time with Cecilia and how—despite several microadventures—our time together was framed by conversation exploring everything from the challenges of her current job to her long-term dreams. Months later, in a reflection I asked her to write as I was working on this project, she mentioned that it was on this trip that I first began talking about writing a book. She also shared this with me:

> Daddy Days are so much more than just a day where you get to choose an activity that Daddy pays for and would normally never do otherwise. They represent a bond being strengthened between the giver and the receiver. . . . My dad has been an exemplary father figure to all of us. Even those who are not his kids look up to him with great admiration. Why do I say this? Well, simply put, I hope to continue this tradition with my own children someday.

Cecilia and I completed one of the Herndon Escape Rooms on the Daddy Day that inspired me to write this book.

Cecilia has always inspired me to make things happen. It's no surprise, then, that I opened my computer and began typing the first paragraphs of what would ultimately become *Daddy Days* on that Sunday evening. My goal was to produce something rooted in my own experience that could be a tool for young parents. And as I began verbalizing this mission early on, the concept slowly became reality. Each time that I had an opportunity to bend the ear of a father about this, they would express enthusiasm, and many have promised me they will start this tradition with their children, as well. Some already have.

As I was nearly finished writing this book, I received a text message from Cecilia regarding her Daddy Day for the year. She proposed we go skydiving. I've skydived previously, once with Maria and again with Renée, Carlos, and Halli a few years later. It is terrifying. But how could I say no? After all, Cecilia helped inspire me to take a metaphorical jump and start writing. She *makes* things happen, and I like to think I do, too. Together, we'll take that jump. We'll share the memory forever.

Acknowledgements

The pain was nine out of ten. My body was screaming all over. It was 11 P.M. on a Friday night in January 2010. I lay in a fetal position on the hard-packed snow below the monster ski jump I just attempted at Crotched Mountain, one of the few places where you can ski so late. I quickly made a deal with God that if he let me walk again, I would dedicate my life to all things good. A crowd quickly formed around me. Ski patrol whisked me into the lodge, where Carlos called Renée at home and told her that I had been seriously hurt. Renée didn't believe him, but when a ski patroller grabbed the phone and told her I was headed to the hospital via ambulance, she got the message.

I had dislocated my right hip, cracked my pelvis, broken my scapula, busted my helmet, destroyed my skis, and shattered my ego. Three hours after the accident, I self-relocated my hip, and with a loud pop the pain went from nine to three. Thankfully, I'd be able to recover from all the injuries.

I first owe an acknowledgement to God for keeping me alive and in one piece that night. I've been blessed in so many ways, and writing this book is part of the oath I made to God after the ski accident. I'm indebted to the main characters in this book: My father, Charles Turner; my wife, Renée Delgado-Turner; my living children: Maria Felicita Schappler, her husband John, their son Andrew John; Carlos Anthony Turner and his wife Halli Rose Underhill; and Cecilia Elena Turner.

My kids have been a source of unbounding joy in my life, and the stories I shared in this book represent only a sliver of the time we spent growing together as a family. The memories are quite literally countless, and I'm proud to say that we will undoubtedly create more even though they are grown.

As I introduced the idea of writing *Daddy Days* to my family members, they each agreed that it was worthy of the effort—an effort that would be enormous. Renée in particular was incredibly supportive and patient during the late nights and long hours I devoted to writing—in addition to working a full-time job and making time for recreation. Renée also bought me *Endangered Species* by David Goethel. It's a superb read by another New Hampshire boat-loving guy who was inspired to write a book after an injury. David introduced me to his publisher, Deidre Randall of Peter E. Randall Publisher in Portsmouth, New Hampshire.

Deidre challenged me to enlist a professional editor. I initially went to a peer, Gary Bouchard, professor of English at Saint Anselm College. Gary reminded me that his son, Jay, a Colorado-based journalist and editor (and new husband and father), may be a better fit for my adventure-filled story. Working with Jay has been pure joy. He expressed incredible enthusiasm for the entire project and our philosophy of life is well matched. I'd be hard pressed to tell you which sentences I cranked out and which are his. Jay gives me hope that the tradition my father started will resonate in a younger generation.

Deidre also introduced me to John Klossner, whose illustrations are on the cover and in the pages of this book. He is a terrific artist whose work reminds us that Daddy Days should always be fun. There are two others worthy of particular mention. It was my sister Sue that first challenged me to create lessons from each story. This helped my writing transition from memoir to relationship guide. David Visco, a business genius, also gave me critical feedback to make the book a more sprightly read.

About the Authors

John (a.k.a. JT or "Rock Iron") Turner is known for his energy, generosity, adventurous spirit, and capable can-do attitude. While the adventures that inspired this book start with his role as son and then dad, it also extends into his roles as husband, family member, business owner, mentor, colleague, and friend. In addition to all his other ventures, John serves as a volunteer firefighter in his community. John's many interests and passions range from engineering design, sailing, hiking, and backcountry and downhill skiing. After a decade of preparations, John and his wife Renée recently opened a Christmas tree farm focusing on building special family experiences, combining his love of the outdoors, children, and faith.

John graduated from University of Maine with his bachelor of science in engineering. He earned multiple engineering licenses (architectural and electrical engineering) early in his career. He is a National Pro-Board-Certified Firefighter. He has held a variety of leadership positions in Business Network International, various Catholic Churches, Amherst Fire Rescue Association, and the Knights of Columbus. He is currently serving on the New Hampshire Diocesan Real Estate and Capital Projects Committee.

John and Renée have three living children: Maria, Carlos, and Cecilia. Maria is married to John Schappler and Carlos is married to Hallie Underhill. John and Renée became grandparents in 2023 with the birth of Andrew John Schappler.

Jay Bouchard is a Denver-based journalist, writer, editor, and teacher. Born and raised in New Hampshire, he moved west to attend Carroll College in Helena, Montana, before earning a master's degree in journalism from Northwestern University. Over the past decade, his writing has been published in *Outside* magazine, *TIME*, *SKI* magazine, *Backpacker* magazine, and many other publications. He spent several years as an editor at *5280*, Denver's award-winning city-regional magazine, and now teaches writing courses while working as a full-time freelance journalist and editor. Like Turner, Jay is an enthusiastic skier, sailor, and all-around outdoorsman at home in the natural world. As a new dad, he can most often be found enjoying the blessings of the Rocky Mountains and New England with his wife and daughter.